LEADING

STARTS IN THE

MIND

LEADING
STARTS IN THE
MIND

Moneim El-Meligi

 **World Scientific**

NEW JERSEY • LONDON • SINGAPORE • BEIJING • SHANGHAI • HONG KONG • TAIPEI • CHENNAI

Published by

World Scientific Publishing Co. Pte. Ltd.

5 Toh Tuck Link, Singapore 596224

USA office: 27 Warren Street, Suite 401-402, Hackensack, NJ 07601

UK office: 57 Shelton Street, Covent Garden, London WC2H 9HE

Library of Congress Cataloging-in-Publication Data
El-Meligi, A. Moneim, 1923–
    Leading starts in the mind : humanistic view of leadership / Moneim El-Meligi.
      p. cm.
    Includes bibliographical references and index.
    ISBN 981-256-413-6 -- ISBN 981-256-495-0 (pbk.)
     1. Leadership. 2. Leadership--Psychological aspects. 3. Organizational behavior.
    4. Management--Psychological aspects. I. Title.

    HD57.7.E4 2005
    658.4'092--dc22

                         2005053898

British Library Cataloguing-in-Publication Data
A catalogue record for this book is available from the British Library.

Printed in Singapore by World Scientific Printers (S) Pte Ltd

To my brothers and sisters in Egypt

Acknowledgements

What is written here has been the product of dialogues with thousands of university students in Egypt and the USA and thousands of managers and leading figures who attended my seminars around the world. I am deeply indebted to all of them. I would like to thank Professor Emeritus Milton Schwartz for the faith he has shown me and for taking the risk in introducing me to my first involvement with management despite my initial resistance.

The old JP Morgan was the first institution to take the risk of launching my Organization Management Seminars. I am deeply grateful to Morgan participants for their trust in my relevance despite the fact that I was then a stranger to the management community. Twenty years of uninterrupted dialogues with them helped shape my views about social systems and the challenge of managing institutions in modern times. I was blessed by the fact that they were very different from me in upbringing, experience and values and yet I could freely express my views. Although I cannot thank all of them individually here, I would like to express my gratitude through those who continued the dialogue with me to this day: Robert Marino, Suresh Chugh, Arthur Eschenlauer and Richard Cavello.

I am equally grateful to many institutions in Singapore for the appreciation of my teachings and consulting services. Special thanks should go to Lim Ho Kee for introducing me to both Singapore and Malaysia, thus widening my world view. I was also most fortunate to have come across Joe Pillay, a magnificent soul who amazed me by the most diversified talents and managerial know-how in presiding over fine institutions such as Singapore Airlines and the Development Bank of Singapore. Three other Singapore leaders deserve my gratitude for their continued interest in my work, Khoo Teng Chye, Lee Ek Tieng and Fock Siew-wah. Special thanks should go to three Human Resources experts in Singapore: Chang Siew Khang and Lam Kai Wah for immortalizing parts of my Organization Management Seminar on DVD, and Jeya Ayadurai who, for more than a decade, coordinated my seminars and consulting activities in various organizations.

For the last twenty years, more than two thousand managers from various institutions in Singapore participated in my seminars. They played an essential role in helping me to formulate and develop ideas on which this book is based. They offered me the gift of listening and kept pressure on me to make my teachings available to the general public in this book and, God willing, in others to come.

I should not forget the continued friendship of Shukri Ibrahim and his wife Som Haji Nor for introducing me to the Malay culture and particularly for their continued efforts to make my seminars available to leaders of the government of Malaysia.

For the manuscript itself, my thanks go to Constantine Vidrenko for her help in the use of computer technology in writing this book, and Susan Miller for reflecting my thinking back to me through Power Point technology. I an equally grateful to all the assistance I got from the Leadership Center of Temasek in Singapore under the guidance of the Center's manager, Tracy Lee. Special thanks should go to three of her staff: Siew Lee Loke, Sharon Chua, and Michelle Chah for many rescue operations whenever I got into trouble with the use of computers whether in conducting my seminars or in writing this manuscript.

I would like to thank Yap Geau Peck for introducing me to World Scientific Publishing. I have been blessed by my editor Kim Tan for her patience and tolerance of my idiosyncrasies. I cannot thank her enough for her efforts and assistance in getting this book published.

A. M. E.
Singapore, October 2005

CONTENTS

LEADING
STARTS IN THE
MIND

INTRODUCTION

And the mind — may God preserve you — is more prone to deep sleep than the eye. Neediest of sharpening than a sword, poorest to treatment, fastest to change, its illness, the deadliest, its doctors, the rarest, and its cure, the hardest. Whoever got a hold of it, before the spread of the disease, found his sake. Whoever tried to wrestle it after the spread would not find his sake. The greatest purpose of knowledge is the abundance of inspiring thoughts. Then, the ways to go about one's needs are met.

— Al-Jahiz[1]

My Involvement in Management

I do not belong to the field of management whatever it may be. My involvement in management occurred as a coincidence. A colleague of mine, himself an authority in the field of "Organization Behavior" invited me to participate in a program he has been in charge of. Apparently he believed that participants in his program who were managers in a large corporation could get "the benefit of my expertise in psychology". I surrendered to his wish after much attempts to convince him of my irrelevance. In my first encounter with managers, I admitted my ignorance without hesitance or shame. I knew then that recognition of ignorance is a gain of knowledge. Naively, I thought

---

[1] Al-Jahiz (9th Century Baghdad), *Kitab at-Tarbi' wat-Tadweer* ("Squaring the Circle"), p. 101. Edited by Charles Pellat, Institut Français de Damas, 1955.

that management had much to do with people and dealing with people was my job as a psychologist. Right from the start I decided to approach the problems of the field as a psychologist. I never felt the need to alter my professional identity. After all, people are people. For a psychologist, it does not matter much whether they were patients in a mental hospital or convicts in a prison, teachers or students in a school, leaders or followers, executives or laborers on assembly line. People, I thought, could be producers or consumers, doctors or patients, liberals or conservatives. I dealt with all such classes of people and, I thought, I could deal with managers or leaders. After all, they too are people aren't they?

I was clearly conscious of my being a stranger among businessmen. Naturally, while sharing my experience as a psychologist, I set out to learn about the functions of a banker or a production engineer. I was curious about the life of a sales person, and intrigued by the character of securities traders. I wondered how a bank teller or an accountant could tolerate going through the same routine activities day in and day out. I wondered how the label "leader" could apply equally to a president of a country, a CEO of a corporation, a principal of a school, an army general, a prison warden, a head of a charity organization, and a football coach. Hundreds of questions would explode in my mind from time to time, enough to shake my confidence in my relevance.

Fortunately, I was armed by an early education in philosophy followed by training in the scientific methodology and administration of instruments. These, I believed, should help me cope initially and also learn about the challenges facing professionals in fields so different from mine. I was thrilled that despite being the expert I thought I was in psychology, I had the chance for fresh learning. So I added to my tasks as a qualified psychologist the burden of being a participant observer. What a thrill it has been to be able to learn while teaching!

What I thought was a limitation turned out to be a blessing. I had no other choice than approaching executives with an open mind. I was authentic in sharing my experience with my audience. I had to learn through face-to-face interaction with thousands of executives and in different cultural settings around the world. Furthermore, failing satisfactory answers to nagging questions that kept popping up in my mind, I had to conduct my own mini research to find instant answers to such pressing questions.

Fortunately, my early training in Egypt as a psychologist took place within the philosophical tradition. That helped me detect philosophical foundations of management theories thought to be new when in fact they may have originated in Plato or Aristotle. Furthermore I was in the habit of gleaning philosophical and the socio-cultural implications of any theory or technique which I came across in my readings. My stance as observer and enquirer, originally due to my being a stranger, became my greatest asset. I simply observe and ask questions and encourage my audience to express their first-hand experience of the issues they were interested in. My seminars impressed my audience around the world as being provocative, not what they expected, fresh (different from the familiar management seminars) and helpful in self understanding and close to common sense. I would give answers to questions that seemed shockingly simple or even naïve. I would like to share below a vintage of my early experiences.

1. Startling Experiences

Teaching an Old Horse

One of the earliest memories comes to mind. That was my first encounter with American managers in a residential program at Rutgers University in New Jersey. Participants were seasoned middle managers from a large reputable corporation. Many of them were veterans of WWII or the Korean War. Soon after I started talking, one participant interrupted in a challenging tone, "Doc, you cannot teach an old horse new tricks." Startled by a self-deprecating remark uttered by an impressive looking executive, I looked around the room as if searching for a proper response. All I could see was a group of executives that seemed equally surprised by the remark. What I saw inspired my response, "I see no horses in this room and I do not play tricks either." There was unanimous laughter, but that incident got me thinking subsequently about several issues — executive training programs, how much an executive is ready to lead and how corporations prepare executives for participation in training programs. Interestingly, at that time I was using the expression adult education. Further acculturation replaced it by management training, the most unfortunate change which was associated with a parallel change, namely replacing the honorable term educator or teacher by trainer.

Another anecdote comes to mind. I was running a seminar for AT&T executives at the invitation of Rutgers University. Apparently, the director of the program had allowed a Human Resource Director from another corporation to sit in as observer throughout the proceedings. At the end of the session, this guest approached me with much enthusiasm. He asked if I would accept to run a similar session for his corporation. I asked him about the purpose of the proposed program. His answer was: I want you to get these managers to *"tear each other apart"*. That was in the sixties, the era of sensitivity training, self awareness and assertiveness training workshops. "Executives tearing each other" sounded bizarre, even obscene. This is because the gist of my presentation has been clearly humanistic. I was also openly critical of excessive self revelation so popular in training programs of the time. He seemed to have been carried away more by the positive reaction of the audience than by the content of the presentation. In fact the aim of my program was to offer means of conflict detection and various strategies for conflict resolution. I pointed this out to him. To his disappointment and surprise, I turned down his invitation. That was one more deep experience to be stored in the depths of my consciousness for the future emergence of my conceptualization of leadership concept.

How about Maslow?

My mind springs forward to the decade of the eighties and from the US to Malaysia. I see myself in a class of managers lecturing on work motivation. I was stressing the point that we can learn a lot about motivation by soliciting workers' immediate experience when someone in the audience protested: "How about Maslow's hierarchy of needs?" Startled by the irrelevance of the remark to what I was talking about, I replied: "How about Maslow's hierarchy?" "You did not mention Maslow's theory," the speaker persisted. To reassure him, I said, "You already know about it. I was talking about the life experience of workers. I was not concerned with theories." He did not seem satisfied. He could not understand how I could eschew talking about such an important theory. It turned out that the questioner had attended a course where he learnt for the first time that needs are structured in a hierarchy from the most primitive physiological needs to the lofty need for self realization. To him, a theory describes a real structure such as a building, not a conceptual interpretation of motivational development. I did know about the theory, but the focus of my talk was about the sources of any theory, observations and experiences. I was also aware of some implications of the theory. If we extrapolate from the hierarchy of needs in individuals to cultural groups we get a similar hierarchy of cultures from the most primitive where people are driven almost exclusively by physiological needs to the most civilized who reached the apex of human evolution reflected in self realization. I had my qualms about a theory with such ethnocentric implications that may contradict Professor Maslow's humanistic philosophy. The important issue here is the habit of passive learning that we should guard against, particularly in leadership training programs.

I Am OK You're OK

While being with the issue of passive learning, I would like to report another incident. I had just finished a lecture in Singapore and as I was hurriedly leaving the lecture hall, a Japanese manager who happened to be a participant in another seminar, caught up with me. He bowed and with the usual Japanese courtesy asked, "Professor, are you teaching 'I am OK, you're OK.'?" He was referring to Eric Burn's technique of Transactional Analysis, quite in vogue at the time in South East Asia. I replied: "No, I don't." Noting his disappointment, I added reassuringly, "It is a very useful approach to human interpersonal communication", and I meant what I said. To this gentleman, leadership training has been reduced to a single approach to communication that in turn has been reduced to a slogan, 'I am OK, You're OK."

These early incidents indicated clearly that many management seminars seem to revolve around the latest fashionable ideas. The media jump upon these ideas and proceed to popularize them with much sensationalism. Soon afterwards, corporations in their eagerness to innovate and compete follow suit. Being too busy, senior managers usually do not have the time to submit such ideas to careful scrutiny, let alone consider their philosophical and practical implications. They send their people in droves to seminars that promote the innovative ideas. Carried away by enthusiasm, those who had the great fortune to attend these seminars return to their respective organizations eager to apply the new knowledge. I once overheard a manager talking about his boss who had just returned from a workshop: "here we go again; he will try a new toy."

2. Case Study

I would like to present a mini case study showing the dilemma of a management consultant in a Third World Country. Government agencies calls on the consultant to solve problems bureaucratic authorities are not equipped to solve or, at least, are too busy to tackle them. The consultant becomes an escape valve as it were. I limit myself to three incidents in which this consultant has been involved. I must add that this consultant is an honorable man with goodwill and has no objection to my presenting his case.

First incident

The government noted that top civil servants in the country are under tremendous pressure from an overly energetic prime minister. Solicitous of the overworked administrators, a high official got this "bright idea": to form an association of wives of top civil servants. The mission of the association was to provide support to their over-worked husbands. Once the organization has been formed, the wives now needed training in leadership, thought the official. The task of training the wives was assigned to my *"management trainer"* friend. As usual, he came to me for informal guidance. He put the problem to me in a very candid and direct manner: "What should I say to the wives?" Surprised by the question, I said: "I really don't know. I do not see how instructing these wives on leadership would have anything to do with the issue of supporting their overworked husbands." Nevertheless he persisted in pressuring me, I told him humorously, "I can only approach these ladies as an experienced husband and not as a professional psychologist and you can certainly do like-wise. You yourself are an overworked husband. Besides, you have no choice since you got yourself into this hole."

Second incident

The government decided to launch a campaign to propagate a "culture of cleanliness". Note the intrusion of the word "culture", a term derived from a scientific discipline, anthropology. "Culture of cleanliness" sounds more impressive than plain cleanliness. And since we are dealing with culture, the authority thought, we have to call on an "expert" in leadership development. As usual, the assignment fell on my friend, a good soldier who never turns down an assignment. And who would he seek but myself, his primary target. It took me some effort to convince him that my expertise does not extend to cleaning public toilets and bathrooms. However, I decided to offer genuine advice because the issue in this case is cleanliness which concerns environmental protection, an issue I feel strongly about. Here are in brief terms the items of my advice: (a) recruit a group of volunteer students from several universities and get the government to equip them with brooms, decent uniforms and all the necessary equipment. (b) Under your direction, the students would then go from one public place to another demonstrating their zeal. (c) Try to get television networks to publicize the occasion. I added: "This will be a great opportunity for you to put your expertise in leadership to the best use. Stop *talking* about leadership, just *lead*." The idea did not appeal to my friend. He thought I was kidding when I was dead serious. Obviously, it is much easier to talk about leadership than practising it.

Third incident

"My problem this time is certainly within your expertise and I need your help," said my friend in anticipation of my usual critical remarks. He had been invited to lecture on communication in a leadership development workshop. I asked him, "Do you have a dictionary of your native language?" He replied, "Yes I do." I told him: "Look up the following words in the dictionary: talk, listen, ramble, gossip, squeal, spy, insinuate, rumor, secrecy, lie, argue, stammer, stutter, convince, persuade, seduce, negotiate, etc. etc." I then added, "If you put down on paper the definitions of these words given in your dictionary and arrange them in a meaningful way, a coherent lecture will emerge and in your own mother tongue." My friend looked intrigued for a moment but soon afterwards he protested: "but that would be *simplistic.*" I retorted: "*Simple* would be the appropriate word."

Like many intelligent and educated professionals, my friend was under the impression that science requires the use of terms that have nothing to do with living. According to them knowledge can only be found in books, preferably those written in English, and true knowledge is brought from books to the world not the other way round. In fact it is the aim of science to provide the simplest answers to our questions. There is also a tendency towards romanticizing science. A case in point is the recent rise of the concept of split brain in South East Asia, implying that creativity resides in the right hemisphere of the brain. Millions of dollars were poured into seminars advocating more use of the right brain, a quantum jump from brain research to applications in adult education. Scientists do not share such attitude towards science. Polykarp Kusch, a Nobel Laureate states that there is no 'scientific method' and what is called by that name can be outlined for only quite simple problems. Another Nobel Laureate, Percy Bridgman, goes even further than Kusch when he said: "There is no scientific method as such, but the vital feature of the scientist's procedure has been merely to do his utmost with his mind, *no holds barred.*"[2]

Misuse of the Term Style

I noticed in my contacts with managers that once a person ascend to a leadership position people view everything he says or does as a leadership act. In one of my seminars I was talking about leadership styles. One participant, a middle level official in the government of a Third World country reported the following incident: his boss, a top civil servant summoned him into his office. As soon as he entered the boss' office, the boss went on reprimanding him for a variety of things. Standing erect in front of the boss, the manager tried to defend himself. Instead of listening, the boss interrupted him, "Go, go, I don't like your face." Feeling morally indignant, the manager calmly but

---

[2] William S. Beck. *Modern Science and the Nature of Life,* New York: Harcourt Brace, 1957.

forcefully retorted: "Sir, if you don't like my face, there is nothing I can do about it. If you don't like my work, I would be glad to receive your instructions. Good day sir." And he left with a sense of vindication. The most interesting thing is that upon hearing what the manager said to his boss, the entire class applauded. Why would they applaud? I asked myself. They too, I guessed, must have been through a similar experience and that the action of their colleague represented a model that they did not dare to live by.

But the main point I wanted to make about this incident is that the manager referred to the behavior of his boss as an example of what is meant by autocratic style of leadership, so prevalent in the civil service in many countries. That gave me the opportunity to point out a serious misunderstanding of the term "style". Leadership style presupposes a consistent pattern of *leadership* behavior. I had to point out that the behavior of this boss had nothing to do with leadership. The boss in this situation stepped out of the leadership role altogether behaving instead as a thug. Meanwhile, he completely ignored the formal role of his subordinate as a leader in his own right, let alone being a grown-up and honorable citizen.

Manager or Leader?

There is a question I always expect to get in the course of teaching whether in university classes or in management seminars. This question is, "what is the difference between a manager and a leader?" I usually throw the question back to the questioner and invite the audience to offer an answer. Invariably, vehement debate ensues without ever culminating by consensus. Arguments and counter-arguments reach a high pitch necessitating my intervention. It became clear to many others in the audience that the same words mean different things to different people. I usually put an end to the arguments by referring the audience to the dictionary to look up the verbs, "to lead" and "to manage" and not the nouns "leader" and "manager". Only then, I thought, would they realize that the habit of using the nouns fixes one's mind on particular persons while the verbs refer to the actions a given person performs. Using the verb or the verbal noun we come to realize that the two sets of activities under the headings "leading" and "managing" overlap a great deal. In other words, the activities determine what label best fits the activities. Later, I required individual participants of any of my seminars on the subject to record their own definitions of both terms and decide whether they think of them as the same thing or two different concepts. Thus, I accumulated a large number of responses the results of which I will discuss later in this book.

Corporate Culture

Corporate culture is one of the topics that comes up frequently in the course of my teaching to graduate students, executives, or educators. The word culture is used so often that people, me included, have assumed that the concept has the same connotation in the minds of different people. This has been the case until a memorable incident took place. I was conducting a workshop to top leaders of a striving corporation and, I must add, a very successful one. Frequent references to "our culture" seemed to irritate one of the participants. He blurted, "hey guys, you keep saying *our culture*. I do not really know what *our culture* is." Most participants were surprised by their colleague's public admission of 'ignorance'. His statement ushered a barrage of definitions. Almost every participant volunteered his own definition or rather, definitions, with great confidence. Fascinated by the controversy I let the discussion go on. It lasted no less than one hour and yet the group failed to reach consensus. I put an end to the discussion by a comment: "There may be a culture there, but we never really cared to share the definition of the term *culture*." Next meeting, I came to the class equipped with a list of nine definitions of the word 'culture' from the Random House Dictionary. I projected the list on a screen. I then invited participants to choose one or more of the list that "best describes the definition of the term 'culture' as you actually use it" which they did. A smooth discussion ensued culminating in agreement on the following two definitions:

❖ The sum total of ways of living built up by a group of human beings and transmitted from one generation to another.
❖ The behaviors and beliefs characteristic of a particular social, ethnic, or age group.

Interestingly, one participant added one more definition — "*the raising of plants or animals, especially with the view to their improvement.*" This participant, it turned out, was originally trained as a botanist. His reason for favoring this definition without refuting the other two was, "it emphasizes the role of the corporation as environment that should enable employees to blossom and grow." That incident and many others cemented my belief that controversy that rages around leadership or any other issue could never be settled unless we share the definition of the words we use. This prompted me to explore the cross-cultural vocabulary pertaining to the concept of leadership. I devoted one of the chapters in this book to leadership semantics.

Empowerment Is the Solution

A decade ago, I noticed the rise of the word "empowerment" in management circles, both in governments and corporations. Faced with acute problems, central among these were the so-called *dead wood*, lowered productivity and turnover of the better employees, organizations seem to have found a *cure* for these problems. The cure is called *empowerment*. What empowerment means in concrete terms, I do not really know. The term is too abstract to suggest specific operational changes. Generally speaking what the promoters of the new movement had in mind was to *grant* subordinates the right to make more decisions. This is a subject that troubled me a great deal. It raised in my mind many questions: how to define empowerment in operational terms? How could empowerment granted from the top down alter the current authority structure? I thought at the time that the real issue lies in something more serious than power differential, namely the philosophy underlying such differential. That set me thinking about the meaning of organizational *membership* and the roles of each member relative to the organization's global mission, or purpose. A lot of thinking and readings I went through yielded a discussion of this topic in this book.

I Want to Be a Great Leader

Frequent encounters with young managers around the world provided me with ample opportunities to unravel considerable number of untested assumptions that underlie their behavior and career aspirations. A case in point: a young manager approached me to find out if he had "all it takes to make a great leader". I asked him, "What for?" "I just want to be a great leader." "What sort of people would you like to lead?", I asked. "It doesn't matter, any people," he replied. I posed another question, "And what would you like to do then?" "Just run a big operation, a corporation or something," he replied. Evidently, leadership in this manager's mind has no content. It is just a compelling vision of him somewhere at the top of a mass of people, an egocentric ambition or indeterminate fantasy. The word "leader" invokes in his mind images of world leaders, historical figures or heroes. Social reformers or activists in non-political domains may also come to mind but less often. Obviously, I thought, false assumptions about leadership contaminate the thinking of young aspirants for leadership positions. Unhealthy leadership practices derive directly from such assumptions, often associated with passionate shallow ambition. Egocentric aspirations have to be dealt with in the selection and training of future leaders. This became paramount in my teaching. I hope that this book will shed some light on this issue.

Recruitment Blunders

Untested assumptions about leadership intrude into recruitment practices. A former student of mine, a human resource specialist, invited me to sit as observer in an employment interview she was about to conduct. Right from the very start of the interview, she assumed an adversary attitude towards the young candidate, challenging him in an unduly aggressive manner. This came as a shock to me because her attitude was at variance with her usual solicitous attitude towards her immediate subordinates. After the interview, I asked her why she was so aggressive. "I was trying to find out if the candidate had leadership potential."

Three assumptions seem to underlie the interviewer's conduct: first, that leadership is somehow related to the ability to aggress, confront, compete or dominate; second that if the candidate fails to manifest these traits in the interview situation, they would not be part of his personality. This would justify turning him down. Third, a bellicose approach by the interviewer is the best *tactic* to elicit leadership potential. Carried away by these assumptions, the interviewer ignored the value implications of her conduct. She ignored that the candidate is already a socialized adult. It would be perfectly natural that he presents himself in a socially desirable manner. Even if he were aggressive *by nature*, he would do his utmost to control his belligerence. That would be a sign of self-control, an attribute that I think would be an asset in a leader. Fourth, the interviewing showed little interest in the ability of the candidate to fit in the organization as an ordinary member, an attribute that should be considered. After all, I thought, *membership precedes leadership.*

While we are on the subject of employment interviews, I would like to relate another situation in which I have been involved, not as an observer, but as a reference for a candidate. The candidate had applied to a middle level position in one of the major banks in the US. Naively, I believed that by recommending the candidate, I was doing a great service to the organization, gratis mind you. The candidate was a former student of mine. He happened to be one of the best graduate students I have ever encountered. To my surprise, the candidate's application was turned down. The reason why the interviewer turned him down was that the candidate still lived with his father. Living with the father at such mature age, thought the interviewer, is a sign of dependency and passivity. Evidently, the interviewer concluded without further enquiry that the candidate could not compete or lead. Had the interviewer enquired a little further than he did, he would have found out that the candidate's father was a widower. As a son, the candidate felt responsible for taking care of him. Furthermore, living with his father did not prevent him from going about his activities in the most productive way. His activities ranged from mountain climbing, skiing trips, travels around the world besides being an art collector and highly cultured individual. Equally surprising, the interviewer ignored the fact that in his previous job, the candidate was responsible for managing a budget of four billion US dollars. This is a case of filial piety taken as impediment without placing a single fact within a broader context. By the way, the interviewer was in charge of Human Resources. He got his job because he was a marine that had mastered the art of killing Asians. No wonder he rejected a candidate as "a soft specimen of renaissance man", to use the interviewer's words.

Elitist View of Leadership

Writers and laymen alike focus predominantly on leaders occupying high authority positions in a nation or in a firm. They are mostly interested in people who have been able to acquire power and have reached the highest offices. There is scarcity of writing about effective leadership among ordinary people in various spheres of social life. There are great leaders nobody hear about nor will ever hear about: school headmasters; head nurses; mother superiors; first line supervisors; school teachers that shun promotions preferring to remain in the classroom; restaurant chefs that run their kitchens like commanders in the heat of battle, dealing with emergencies under tremendous pressure from demanding clients and harassed waiters; student leaders; social service workers in neighborhoods plagued by crime, drug abusers and drug dealers; ex-convicts that succeed where the prison system has failed in either rehabilitation of offenders or in crime prevention.

3. Writing This Book

William James

As I set out to write this book, I found myself under the spell of my early experience lecturing to managers or graduate students of management. As William James once said, "Facts have coercive power." But the above anecdotes, mundane as they may appear to some, constituted an insidious program of education for me. I grew up and received my education in Egypt and later in England. I worked first in Egypt and later in the US, but since the seventies I lead a nomadic life around the world with frequent and long sojourns in South East Asia, particularly Singapore. So naturally the influence of various cultures must have penetrated deeply into my psyche. I would naturally approach problems from various angles — primarily as a psychologist, albeit critical of his own discipline, often as anthropologist with much interest in cultural differences and commonalities, but also the philosopher in me watching over to ponder the wider implications of my observations and assertions. When faced by a puzzling issue for which I found no ready answer in the literature, I would resort to simple research. In my research I simply pursued my "chronic" experiential approach which dominated my early work in the study of mental disorders. The central position in this work has been the emphasis on immediate experience. After all, leadership is not only behavior to observe but is also an intimate living experience that envelops the leaders and followers alike.

Information Overload

In the course of this insidious education, I found out that the field of management suffers from congestion and informational overload. Difficult problems of terminology, method, and theoretical formulations beset it from all its sides. I came to the conclusion that the pressing need is not for more facts or more data but for conceptual schemes and systematic theories into which we may fit the facts we have, and the facts we shall gather in the future. The incidents I cited above got me thinking that the problem with leadership does not reside in lack of leadership skills or leadership potential but in the way we think about leadership. So it was natural that the current book revolves around thinking. But how can we think about leadership without considering the language in which we put our thoughts. How could we divorce management literature from consideration of language and form? So, two chapters on semantics seemed necessary. One chapter derives from empirical studies of the meanings which managers assign to the words *leader* and *manager*. The other explores the semantics of leadership in different languages and different cultures. Interestingly, the latter was the first chapter that I felt constrained to conclude before I could venture into the other chapters in the book. I must also add that tackling the semantics of leadership regulated my thinking throughout this entire project.

I was also confronted by another question: how can we think about leadership without thinking about where leadership takes place? It takes place within and between social groups and organizations. Therefore, I had to devote considerable space to the meanings we assign to organizations both as environment and process, to forces of construction and decay in organizations, to a typology of situations that demand different leadership approaches and to individual differences in the perception of, and attitude towards organizations.

Conceptualization of Leadership

Most of the work that has been done on leadership approached the subject from outside. I chose to look at leadership as a mode of existence in relation to other human individuals. Leadership as I saw it is a human endeavor, a relationship that we experience as we engage in it. We cannot talk about leadership in the abstract. For example, if we want to know the criteria of effective leadership, we simply go to people and ask them. They and they alone are able to tell how they think, feel and act when they assume the role of leading others, or when they are required to follow the dictates of another person or when they find themselves in such position that requires them to shift back and forth between the reciprocal roles of leading and following.

No matter where we go, we will find ourselves face to face in a situation where people are giving directions or receiving directions; exerting influence or receiving influence. We will witness someone exercising authority, abdicating authority or abusing it. We will witness a person tyrannizing others or a person that people follow, sometimes blindly and happily. I have always been aware that leadership begins when two parties meet, whether individuals or groups. And when the parties meet, there is life with all its complexity and ambiguity. In short there is more to leadership than a person bossing around someone else. There is more to leadership than just a style or criteria of effectiveness. My conceptualization of leadership challenges much of the traditional notions of leadership. I question, for example, the universality of intelligence, dominance, aggressiveness and extraversion as absolute criteria of leadership effectiveness. Instead of imposing an *ideal* model of leadership, I lay the philosophical foundations that will allow institutions to make their own choice of the model (or models) in the light of their own cultural values and unique historical circumstances. For this reason, this book can best be described as interdisciplinary and a cross-cultural guide for policy making, particularly with regard to the selection, training, and counseling of leaders.

The content of this book is a mix of my first-hand experience, empirical research and readings. In my readings I did not limit myself to what is written in the field of management or even psychology. I sought insight from any source that I thought might shed light on the subject — anthropology, thermodynamics, mysticism, and literature. The book offers various conceptual models that are likely to enhance our ability to diagnose leaders' effectiveness and assess the outcome of leaders' efforts on the performance of the groups or the institutions they lead. Two among the models are worth highlighting. The first, "LFF" explains the dynamic interaction that takes place in the life of a leader among three distinct but interdependent attitudes: *Leadership*, *Followership*, and *Fellowship*. Each of these attitudes constitutes a vital resource for any leader. According to this model, the effectiveness of a leader does not depend exclusively on the will and skill in leading, but on the ability of the leader to shift back and forth among the three attitudes according to the demands of the situations. The second model, *"Leadership Prerequisites"* proposes five major conditions without which leadership potential could not be realized.

Purpose of the Book

I believe that this book will equip readers with the conceptual tools that will enable them to counteract the onslaught of information. It will serve as a guide for thinking about leadership: reveal the underlying assumptions that drive our decisions, policy making and interactions with other fellow human beings. I must admit that I could not in good faith offer a definition of leadership *in itself* for the simple reason that leadership is not *something* that exists *in itself*. I could only conceive leadership as *actions* or *processes* undertaken by individuals and groups in different cultural settings and in different time contexts. Besides, people have different definitions and different criteria for what they consider effective leadership. Furthermore, leadership is more than just a scientific subject of enquiry. It is an integral part of the life of individuals and societies. The scientist is welcome to throw light on its manifestations but it is not the scientist's business to tell people how to conduct their lives.

Finishing the Book

I was learning about the subject from books, from endless dialogues with thousands of participants in my seminars around the world, and from many others that generously accepted to participate as subjects in my various research projects. It took me some time before I could extricate myself from my academic involvement to spell out my thoughts and feelings with as much authenticity as is humanly possible. Finally I must admit that there remain a lot of things that I haven't completely worked out. I hope I will live long enough to pursue what I missed.

Title of the Book

The reader may wonder what I meant by the word "mind" in the title of the book. I do not feel obligated to provide a technical definition. I can only say that I am not talking here about the mind of the philosophers or biologists or psychologists. I hold on to the colloquial usage of the word "mind" in day-to-day encounters: for example, "I mind my own business," "you have been on my mind lately," "I speak my mind," "meeting of the minds," or "you're out of your mind." I mean the mind that I experience directly and that enables me to direct my senses and make sense out of the barrage of sense impressions that I keep getting from the world around me. My mind is what projects me into the unknown through reasoning, fantasy and dreams. It is that force that connects me to the past through memory, to the future through imagination, and to the unknown through intuition. In fact the book could very well be called "Thinking about Leadership".

I have no claim to add something strikingly novel. Writing, or rather trying to write this book has been a decade of learning and trying to understand the issues related to leadership as a universal human phenomenon. In the meantime it was a humbling experience, the experience of a man who wants to understand, to reconcile conflicting views or observations none of which could be denied and to deal with an avalanche of information. In this I adopt David Hume's definition of his role as a philosopher: "*to be employed as an under-labourer in clearing the ground a little, and removing some of the rubbish that lies in the way of knowledge.*"

Leaders or Managers?[3]

Always when any key term is ambiguous or of otherwise indeterminate meaning it becomes imperative that all those introducing that term begin by indicating which sense or what sense they favour; and equally imperative that they remain constant in their fidelity to that choice. For the sociologist, as the Marquis de Vauvenargues insisted it was for the philosopher, "clarity is a matter of good faith."

— Antony Flew[4]

1. First Was the Word

What do you really mean when you utter the word "leader" or "manager"? Meanings of words do not reside in the words themselves, they reside in the minds of people who use them. So let us start exploring the meanings of leadership in the minds of people. It is often said that: "A word is not a crystal, transparent and unchanging; it is the skin of a living thought and may vary greatly in color and content according to the circumstances and time in which it is used."

In the course of teaching about leadership, I am often asked: "What is the difference between a manager and a leader?" The question itself presupposes the presence *in reality* of two distinct types of human beings: managers and leaders. Those who pose the question forget that words are invented by people and that they do not necessarily refer

---

[3] What does the word, "manager" or "leader" trigger in most people's minds?

[4] *Thinking about Social Thinking*, p. 29.

to human beings in flesh and blood. The question shows how people can be prisoners of words they invented. I found that any answer from me is futile. If I say they are synonyms, some people object. If I say they are identical, I get strong objections. Finally I decided to return the question to the questioners and ask them to provide the answer themselves. That led me to start any seminar by a simple questionnaire and ask the participants to put the answer on paper. Here are the questions that I provide on a sheet of paper where participants were required to write down their answers:

> When you use the words "leader" and "manager", do you think of them as two different concepts or as two words that have the same connotation? Indicate your opinion by circling either A or B below. If you think of them as two different concepts, indicate the differences in the respective columns in the table below.
>
>   a. The words *"leader"* and *"manager"* mean more or less <u>the same</u> to me.
>
>   b. The words *"leader"* and *"manager"* have <u>different connotations</u> in my mind.

The reader may like to respond to this questionnaire before going through this chapter. In one of my seminars I asked the participants to respond to the questions above. I collected data from three different groups. The responses are shown in Tables A. B. and C. in Appendix I. In this chapter I will deal with data from the first of these groups. The data represents the responses of those who indicated that the two terms "lead" and "manage" have different meanings in their minds. Out of a class of 20 participants, 15 indicated that the words "leader" and "manager" have different connotation in their minds. The definitions they offered to both terms are shown in Figure 1 below.

FIGURE 1

Managers' view of the differences between the concepts
"leader" and "manager"

Case No	LEADER	MANAGER
1	Always considers subordinates first. Dares to make decision in the absence of fact.	Has a proper path to follow.

Case No	LEADER	MANAGER
2	A leader is able to motivate, initiate something which others may follow. He may be a manager.	A manager has a leader's characteristics. It is important that a manager has a leader's character.
3	Provides strategic direction and guidance. Listens actively to staff grievances and pertinent issues and (escalates) reports to senior management to seek resolution.	Manages a team of staff.
4	Does the right things. Sets the vision and directions of the organization.	Does the thing right. Implements to achieve set objectives. The end justifies the means. Manages resources: time, manpower, materials, budget.
5	A leader can be elected. A leader has followers to lead. A leader leads but not necessarily manages. A leader sounds lower-end.	A manager is appointed. A manager may have subordinates. There are sometimes managers without any subordinates. A manager manages. A manager sounds high-end.
6	A leader is not necessarily a good manager or one who can manage.	A manager can manage but may not have leadership qualities.
7	Visionary, authoritative, eminent, enthusiastic, veto power.	Planner, enterprising, obedient, cautious.
8	Manages the followers or supporters to do right things. Must possess good values in order to lead by example. Total commitment.	Encourages staff to do things right. Have good values but are assertive to carry out instructions. Committed during working hours.
9	A leader to me is always a manager in one form or another. Even in the most mundane activities, a leader will always have some form of managing to do.	A manager is not always a leader.

Case No	LEADER	MANAGER
10	Provides the vision. Determines the "where" and the what. Needs to empower people. Sets direction. Takes risks. Takes uncharted waters. Develops and creates new ideas.	Plans and organizes the implementation of the vision. Determines the now and the "when". Needs to motivate people. Implements direction. Manages risk. Sails on chartered waters. Produces ideas.
11	A good leader portrays a good manager but a good manager does not necessarily portray a good leader. He reflects credibility of the person but in a manager it reflects glamour.	A manager takes most responsibilities formally and requires training as a leader. Lack of leadership skills in the manager results in mismanagement and chaos.
12	A leader is one who possesses attitudes that others around him look to guidance, help and support.	A manager leads as well as: Plans: must have a vision beyond the immediate time frame; Executes: sets, tends towards getting things done and will not accept lack of action when it is needed; Controls: supervises, monitors and obtains feedback so that actions may be amended if necessary.
13	Not necessarily seen as a manager.	Manager must prefer development apart from the normal tasks.
14	Covers a broader perspective. Cares about the welfare of its (sic) employees. Concern about the long-term objectives of the organization. Encourages a two-way communication between all levels. Hold the good values of the organization.	Limited to specific assignments or tasks.

Case No	LEADER	MANAGER
15	A leader is one who has the power to influence another person or group of persons in the way they exercise their choices. The power possessed by the leader is attained either by means of his social status, economy, political, religious, military or even charismatic charm. A leader is not necessarily a manager. A leader leads people; a single person without a follower cannot be a leader; whereas a single person could be assigned as a manager to perform specific function with allocated economic rewards.	A manager is one who is accountable and responsible for specific economic rewards (human, machines, tools, assets, etc.) For the purpose of specific objectives.

2. Interpretation of the Responses

Subject No. 1

Let us examine the responses given by 15 managers in Figure 1. Note that these are among the managers who stated that the two terms "leader" and "manager" refer to different types of people. Respondent no. 1 tells us that a leader "considers subordinates first". Does the respondent imply that a manager *does not* consider subordinates first? And no mention of what comes next. He adds that a leader "dares to make decisions in the absence of facts". What he may have meant was that a leader is characterized by risk-taking and that making decisions in the absence of facts is an asset that differentiates a leader from a manager who just follows a predetermined path.

Subject No. 2

"A leader motivates and initiates". So far the response makes sense. But the next statement "a leader may be a manager" contradicts the initial assertion that leader and manager have different connotations. The respondent goes on to tell us that "it is important that a manager has a leader's character". Conceptual muddle is glaringly evident.

Subject No. 3

The respondent attributes a specific function to a leader, namely "provides strategic direction and guidance". Since he stated at the outset that a leader is different from a manager one would rightly infer that a manager does not provide the same. However, the respondent does not openly say so. Instead he tells us that a manager "*manages* a team of staff". Respondent defines a word by itself. The second response assigns two specific functions to a leader: a) listens to staff grievances, and b) reports them to higher authority for resolution. How about the manager counterpart? No mention.

Subject No. 4

The first response is: "The manager *does the right thing*" in contrast to the manager who "*does the thing right*", a fancy cliché devoid of meaningful information. The second response is clearer: "A leader has the vision and sets direction of the organization while a manager implements, and handles material and manpower." In other words: a leader thinks but the manager just implements.

Subject No. 5

The issue of election comes up for the first time. What distinguishes a leader from a manager is the different ways they come to office. The former is elected while the latter is appointed. A second distinction lies in the fact that a leader has followers but a manager may or may not have subordinates. Then the respondent runs into a problem as he realizes that a leader leads but does not necessarily manage but a manager manages, period.

Subject No. 6

We encounter again glaring conceptual muddle when the respondent tells us that a leader is not necessarily a good manager and that a manager may not have leadership qualities. Why then did the respondent indicate at the outset that the two terms denote different meanings? Here we witness semantic muddle associated with logical confusion.

Subject No. 7

No. 7 offers us a list of adjectives that glorify a leader, cognitive (visionary), emotive (enthusiastic) besides having a high standing (authoritative, eminent and powerful). Another list of adjectives, two of them refer to managerial functions (planning and enterprising) and two suggestive of low status (obedient and cautious). I wonder how the respondent sees himself. All we know from his responses is that it is far better to be called a leader than a manager.

Subject No. 8

We encounter once more the cliché "Doing the right thing" versus "doing things right". The former characterizes the leader while the latter characterizes the manager. It would appear that "doing the right thing" is superior to "doing things right". The last item in the response is interesting: a leader is totally committed but a manager is committed only during working hours.

Subject No. 9

The respondent sees no difference between a leader and a manager.

Subject No. 10

Vision versus implementation comes up again so does the theme of superiority of a leader over a manager. The former sets direction and the latter implements. In other words, a manager is really a follower. Reference to time orientation shows up for the first time in this batch of responses: a leader "determines the *where and the what*" but the manager determines the "*now and the when*". In addition the leader *empowers* people but a manager "*motivates*". Again, a leader is superior to a manager.

This respondent makes the differentiation on the basis of attitude to risk, the leader takes risk but the manager just manages it. Then he adds another unclear difference related to creativity, namely the leader "develops and creates ideas" but the manager "produces ideas". He probably means that the manager implements ideas, careless use of words.

Subject No. 11

Respondent number 11 appears confused by the overlap between the two terms. He seems concerned with what makes a good manager in contrast with a good leader. "A good leader *portrays* a good manager, but a good manager does not *portray* a good leader." The respondent does not explain what "portrays" mean. He becomes even more ambiguous, or maybe, muddled when he adds that "he [?] reflects credibility of the person, but in a manager it reflects glamour". What does the pronoun "he" refers to is anybody's guess. Reference to credibility versus glamour suggests muddled thinking.

Subject No. 12

This respondent brings followers into the picture. A leader is one who have [sic] followers who look to him for guidance, but the manager is one who does things: plans, executes and controls.

Subject No. 13

This participant failed to substantiate his initial claim that the two words have different connotations in his mind. In fact he failed to provide any information.

Subject No. 14

A person whom this participant calls leader "has a wide perspective": cognitively, he "concerns himself with long-term objectives of the organization" and interpersonally he "encourages two-way communication". In contrast a manager is one that limits his activities to specific tasks. In short a leader is superior to the manager on both counts.

Subject No. 15

This participant differentiated between a leader and a manager in terms of power. The former has more influence and attains more power than a manager. He adds "charismatic charm" to the virtues of a leader. He also showed awareness of the literal meaning of the word "leader".

A leader leads people but a manager does not have to. A manager may not even have people to deal with. Finally while the word leader evokes power and influence, the word manager evokes accountability.

3. Summary of the Findings

First, the most striking finding is that participants were more fluent when defining the meaning of the word leader than in defining that of the word manager. The word count of the former category is 336 words compared to 243 words for the latter category.

Second, all attributes ascribed to leader have positive connotations. They assert the leader's superiority to a manager at different levels of functioning. At a cognitive level, a leader is one who "thinks strategically", "builds up support for a vision", "is innovative", "has wide perspective", "focuses on organizational objectives", "plans, directs and guides". The opposite attributes characterize a manager who tends to be "conserving rather than innovating", "deals with specific tasks", and is "more bureaucratic". At an interpersonal level, the leader is "concerned with the well being of people", "encourages interpersonal communication", is more "risk-taking", and may even have "military and charismatic charm". It is evident that all these responses display the subjects' evaluative attitudes that honors a leader and demeans a manager. In view of this attitude, one wonders who would ever want to be called a manager. And yet the respondents were in fact managers and were enrolled in a seminar on management development.

Third, the differences between a leader and a manager become much sharper when the participants make the comparison on the basis of power and influence. A leader "exerts and acquires more power", "is authoritative and eminent", "determines the where and the what", "has power to influence another person or group of persons", "attains power by means of his social status", and "has followers to lead". In contrast a manager "executes", "implements directions", and "carries out instructions". In other words, the word leader evokes ideas of power, authority and independence but the word manager evokes accountability, submission and obedience.

Fourth, some of the responses are either stereotyped slogans or make no sense at all. Examples are:

❖ a leader does the right things

❖ a manager does the things right
❖ a leader sounds lower-end
❖ a manager sounds high-end

Fifth, often participants fail to draw the line between both concepts. Here are some examples:

❖ a leader may be a manager
❖ a manager has a leader's characteristics
❖ a leader is not necessarily a good manager
❖ a manager can manage but may not have leadership qualities

Sixth, the responses given by 15 participants may be summarized by one statement: "A leader is a good boss and a manager is a mediocre one."

4. Theoretical Implications

I must add a word here about the participants who were generous enough to participate in the exercise. They are all middle-level managers, university graduates, and are more-or-less successful in their respective careers. They are eloquent, clear, and rational when they talk to you. But when they put down their responses on paper, they became ambiguous, and sometimes illogical if not incoherent. It seems that talking and writing are two different modalities of communication. It may well be that the discrepancy between the two situations are specific to some common words and should not be generalized to other words. Participants may have always used these two words assuming that they were somehow different but have never really thought about the difference nor have they ever cared to test their assumptions against other people's thinking.

I advise the reader to inspect the responses I gathered from the other two groups, B and C in Appendix I. I decided to spare the reader the boredom of going through the whole lot because I thought that the current sample is fairly representative of the entire population. The reader may arrive at the same conclusions that I arrived at but may also find other features that I missed.

Personally, I have no quarrel with using any word as long as the user tells me what the word means. The term leadership is often used in a very loose and general sense to group together indiscriminately a vast array of behavior tendencies and personality traits. I took pains to pursue with increasing specificity the various dimensions of what people loosely call leadership. After all, meanings of words do not reside in the words themselves but in the minds of people who use them. Either term is a label we choose among many others to refer to a person holding or assuming a given position or enacting a given role. So the choice of the term is a matter of convenience. It is arbitrary. We must bear in mind that when we use either term we are no longer talking about an abstract position but about a *holder* of a position. Our focus should be on the functions that a person is supposed to fulfill, what he actually does, and how he or she goes about fulfilling it.

When my grandson was four years old, he was fascinated by the tools I keep in the drawers of my desk such as a stapler, hole-punching tool, paper cutter, scotch tape, and several other gadgets. He would pick up, say, the stapler and asks, "What does this *do*?" He would then pull the scotch tape and asks, "What does this do?" He picks up one gadget after the other asking the same question about each. Immediately after I tell him what the object *does*, he proceeds to use it with great enthusiasm. Often he discovers other usages it was not invented for For him, the name designates an object that must have a specific function. So it is the function that makes the object relevant to the child. And it is relevant simply because he *intends* to use it. The child knows what semanticists have been telling us all along, that *the name is not the thing*. A name that does not point to a function, an event, or an action is useless. This is as true to an adult as it is to a child. That is why I always advise my students when we talk about a person in a leadership position it would be safer first to use the verbs such as "lead" and "manage" or the verbal noun "leading" and "managing". The verb or the verbal noun has the advantage of referring to observable action occurring in the context of a situation which specifies the time, past, present or future.

Going back to the issue of the differences between manager and leader, what matters is what a person in the position of authority is supposed to do, is expected to do, intends to do, or is actually doing. *Doing* is what defines the holder of a position. If we happen to have two distinct sets of functions, it would be perfectly legitimate to give them two different names. It is equally legitimate to use synonyms to denote the same set of functions.

In any group, formal or informal, we cannot find a particular *slot* to be occupied by a leader and another *slot* for a manager. There is work to be done and we need an individual to be in charge of the work. What that person does will define him or her. And what a person will do is partly determined by the responsibilities assigned to him or her. However, usually the incumbent of a position has a certain margin of freedom. Such margin allows him or her to stress features which another person in a similar position would naturally ignore.

The word leader has acquired more prestige than the word manager. The latter acquired more prestige than the word administrator. The prestige dimmed the importance of many other aspects. During the 1970s, some universities decided to change the name of their schools of *business administration* to schools of *management*. Other schools followed the new trend, the "*me too*" phenomenon. I was at the time Professor at what used to be the Graduate School of Business Administration of Rutgers, the State University of New Jersey. The university decided to adopt the new label. School of Management sounded more respectable. All professors cheered the decision with the exception of one, our eldest. He was indignant. To him the new label was demeaning and even vulgar. After all, he once confided to me, the President of the United States refers to his "Administration", not to his management. Words have different meanings. That we know, but they also have different histories and different prestige. Moreover, the prestige acquired today may be lost tomorrow.

The most valuable lesson I learnt from the exercise I reported above is never to take it for granted when people use the same word that the word means the same thing to every one of us. The study prompted me to explore the concept of leadership in different languages. This I did to the best of my ability benefiting from my familiarity with Arabic, my mother tongue, English, French, and the Malay language. The latter I hardly know, but the dictionaries helped. I included the results of this exploration in the next chapter of the book.

Leadership Semantics
Cross-Cultural Exploration

To perceive how language works, what pitfalls it conceals, what its possibilities are is to comprehend a crucial aspect of the complicated business of living the life of a human being.

— S. I. Hayakawa

1. Comparative Study

Names of leadership positions in different cultures provide a glimpse into the roles the holders of positions are expected to fulfill.

English Language

The list in English is long: administrator, boss; captain, chief, chieftain, commander, conductor, director, executive, foreman, godfather; governor, guide, guru; head, kingpin; magnate, manager, master, mentor, mogul, officer, patriarch, principal, ruler, superior, supervisor, marshal; and much more.

Hierarchical organizations are intent on differentiating leadership roles to indicate variations in authority: Chairman at the top of the list followed by deputy chairman and so on down the line to the first line supervisor. Confusion abounds when the titles are meant to simultaneously convey the authority attached to the position and the functions that the occupant of the position is expected to fulfill. Thus we get the differentiation between the chairman of the firm; the chief executive officer (CEO), the chief operating officer (COO) and, more recently, the chief information officer (CIO).

The list is even longer in the army than in business firms. The term "general" is too general since it applies to any of the five highest ranks: brigadier general, major general, lieutenant general, general, or "general of the army". Similar ambiguity characterizes the title "marshal". The dictionary lists six variations of leadership:

❖ An administrative officer of a US judicial district with duties similar to those of a sheriff.
❖ The chief of a police or fire department.
❖ An official who leads special ceremonies, as a parade.
❖ An army officer of the highest rank, as in France.
❖ A high officer of a royal household or court.

The same word as a transitive verb seems much clearer — it draws our attention to observable actions or events that we can witness:

❖ To arrange in proper or effective order: to marshal facts,
❖ To array, as for battle, or
❖ To usher or lead ceremoniously.

We encounter similar variation of titles in both the ecclesiastical and academic hierarchies. The former Soviet Union consolidated all titles into "comrade" but differentiated incumbents according to the power they wield in the communist party.

While sharing membership with other people in the respective social systems, position holders have specific charge of leading, guiding, commanding, representing, rewarding, hiring or firing, appraising or monitoring. Persons in charge are expected to engage in all or some of those activities. The way they conduct their roles vary according to the individual's temperament and the circumstances surrounding him or her. Superiors' performance has a wide range of influence on their subordinates: compliance, passive obedience, devotion, opposition, sabotage, and many other reactions. In doing what they do, position holders may be perceived as effective or ineffective; inspiring or unexciting; charismatic or rational.

<u>English</u>

Drive (verb)

1. Move, advance; lead, guide, conduct; push forward, spur, urge along.
2. Press, urge, prod, goad; incite, impel.
3. Advance, press forward; rush.

Guide (verb)

1. To assist (a person) to travel through, or reach a destination in an unfamiliar area, as by accompanying or giving directions to the person.
2. To accompany (a sightseer) to show and comment upon points of interest.
3. To force (a person, object, or animal) to move in a certain path.
4. To supply (a person) with advice or counsel.
5. To supervise (someone's actions or affairs) in an advisory capacity; manage.

Guide (noun)

A person who guides, especially one hired to guide travelers, tourists, etc.

Lead [verb, intransitive]

1. To be first; be ahead.
2. To go first as a guide.
3. To act as commander, director, or guide.
4. Command; leadership: took over the lead of the company.
5. To be an example; a precedent: followed his sister's lead in running for office.

Vassal (noun)

1. (In the feudal system) a person granted the use of land in return for rendering homage, fealty, and usually military service to a lord or other superior; feudal tenant.
2. A person holding some similar relation to a superior; a subject or subordinate.
3. A servant or slave.
4. Having the status or position of a vassal.

Vanguard
1. The front part of an advancing army.
2. The forefront in any movement or field.
3. The leaders of any intellectual or political movement.

<u>French</u>

❖	*agir*	to act, to take action
❖	*agitateur*	agitator or ring leader
❖	*censeur*	censor, deputy headmaster
❖	*directeur (m)-rice (f)*	director
❖	*dirigeant*	a person in charge, head, conductor
❖	*diriger, vt*	to run [something], to be in charge of, to be head of, to manage, to supervise
❖	*gérant m,*	director (of a restaurant or a football team)
❖	*gérer*	to oversee, to guide, to direct, to steer, to control, to verify, to organize
❖	*gérer un conflit*	manage conflict
❖	*manier*	hold [by the hand], use, utilize, drive
❖	*mener*	to lead somebody somewhere
❖	*meneur (pejorative)*	agitator
❖	*meneur, euse*	leader
❖	*parrain*	Godfather: a child's godfather, sponsor or promoter of a project, patron [of a charitable affair]
❖	*préfet*	elected mayor or head of police
❖	*proviseur*	headmaster or head teacher

<u>German</u>

❖	*Führer*	guide

<u>Greek</u>

❖	*hegemonía*	leadership, supremacy
❖	*hegemon*	leader
❖	*kar'izuhm*	charisma[5]

---

[5]A special quality conferring extraordinary powers of leadership and the ability to inspire veneration; a personal magnetism that enables an individual to attract or influence people, or a divinely conferred gift or power.

Bahasa Melayu

- ❖ *ketua*, or *kepala*   headman or chief
- ❖ *pemimpin, ketua,*   leader
- ❖ *pengurus* or *pentadbir*   administrator

Bahasa Indonesia

- ❖ memelopori, bertindak   to take the lead in proposing
- ❖ memimpin   to lead an orchestra, troops, or in prayers
- ❖ mengambil   to take the lead in sports event
- ❖ peranan penting   to lead (in a play or film)
- ❖ pimpinan, kemimpinan   leadership
- ❖ pimpinan / bimbingan   to take the lead

It is interesting to note that the Indonesian version of the Malay language varies the term to match the situation where leading takes place. For example, leading an orchestra is denoted by the word *memimpin* while leading in sports is referred to by the word *mengambil*.

Indian

- ❖ *Ni-zām* (noun)   ruler (in Hyderabad from the 18th century to 1950)
- ❖ *Nizām-al-mulk* (Urdu)   governor of the realm

In the Turkish language the same terms denote order. For this reason they are used to refer to a regular army or any member of it. The word is derived from the Arabic language where it means order, system or pattern. Thus whether in Turkish or Urdu, the word shifted attention from the system to the overseer of the system.

Arabic Language

- ❖ *Amir*   prince or commander (from *amr*: issue or command)
- ❖ *Iktid'a*   following the example of someone, copying, imitating, or emulating
- ❖ *Ka'id*   leader, applies mostly to a military person, army general and more recently to an orchestra director
- ❖ *kaddām*   a courageous person

❖   *Kawwād*   This term is an exaggerated derivative of the
                     same root. It indicates a person who is "in the
                     habit of" leading. That term is used in daily
                     discourse to refer to a person who furnishes
                     clients for a prostitute, roughly a panderer or a
                     pimp.
❖   *Kuddām*   ahead of others in terms of status, honor *Sharaf*
                     or authority *riasat*
❖   *M'amūr*   Receiver of the command. This term implies
                     delegated authority. It is derived from the root
                     amr (command or issue). Hence, *m'amūr* is one
                     who is authorized (by a higher authority) to issue
                     commands.
❖   *Mohafez*   Conserver, usually used for mayor of a city or
                     governor of a region. It derives from the root
                     verb *ḥāfaza* or to conserve.
❖   *Motasarref*   dispenser (the person who dispenses)
❖   *Mudir*   derives from the verb *adāra* (to turn something
                     around such as a machine or business of some
                     kind)
❖   *Murakeb*   overseer, derives from the root verb *rākaba*
                     (to monitor or oversee)
❖   *Murshid*   a guide, or a person that shows the way
❖   *Mushrif*   observer or overseer
❖   *Sāiis*   administrator
❖   *Sāsa al 'amal* to manage work or administer a task (used also
                     for grooming or tending to animals)
❖   *Sāsa al kawm* to govern people or rule a community
❖   *Siāsa*   politics
❖   *Siāsi*   politician
❖   *Tadbir*   Tadbir is a noun that derives from the root verb
                     dabbara (to manage but with consideration of
                     consequences, in other words the term has an
                     element of reflection. Thus *tadbir al-manzel* or
                     the effective handling of household affairs.
❖   *Tasarrof*   dispensation
❖   *Tasreef*   dispensing
❖   *za'im*   usually refers to a popular political leader

The words *Tasarrof* and *Tasreef* are nouns that refer specifically to the phase of implementation in management, namely taking action, or getting things done from day to day, hence, *tasreef al omūr*, or the settling of matters. In this sense, the two words complement the concept of *tadbīr* that stresses the cognitive act of reflection or deliberation.

A distinctive property of the Arabic language is worth mentioning at this juncture. Any Arabic word is derived from a root that consists of three consonant letters of the alphabet. From this root, several words could be derived whether they are nouns, verbs or adjectives. Take the word "lead" for example. It is derived from a root of three consonants: K, W and D. These three letters could be arranged in various ways producing different concepts or meanings as the list below shows:

kadā	to lead or guide
Ka'id	leader or general
kawwad	in the habit of leading or pimp
inkada	to be led or guided
inkiad	the act of submitting to someone else
kaddama	to advance or to submit something
takaddama	to proceed, to progress, to go ahead of somebody
koddam	front part or front position
mokaddamat	front part, or introduction of a book

One lexicographer reckons the number of Arabic roots at 19,000, another at some 21,000, each capable through the mechanism of 'derivation' *(ishtiqaaq)*, of creating more than a hundred words. This richness, organized according to precise structures and a rigorous logic, emerged in the age of Charlemagne. Other than through the grammarians themselves, who operated after the event, we scarcely know anything of the preceding stage (Berque, pp. 24, 25).[6]

---

[6] Saussure rightly underlined the importance of what he called the arbitrariness of the sign, namely the fact that no logical connection inherently links the syllables of the word *oiseau* (French for bird), for example, to what they mean. But unlike those of European languages, Arabic words are usually derived in an obvious way from a single root. *Maktūb, mahtab, mahtaba, hātib, kitāb,* for example, are all constructed from a root K. T. B., meaning "to write", whereas French, to denote the same objects, resorts to five words having no connection between them: *écrit, bureau, bibliothèque, secrétaire, livre* (written, office, library, secretary, book), pp. 25, 26.

2. Conclusions

The following conclusions can be drawn from this semantic exercise:

First, the vocabulary currently used in the management literature is impoverished by comparison with the versatility noted in all languages. Only two words prevail in the management literature: "management" and "leadership". Occasionally the word administration pops up.

Second, noun words prevail over verbs or verbal nouns. A noun refers either to a person such as a leader or a manager, or to an abstract concept such as leadership or management. In contrast a verb refers to an act or a concrete event that occurs in the world. As a result the literature focuses on what goes on in the minds of leaders or on their individual differences rather on whether or not they actually lead. When we talk about leadership we think of it primarily as something that a person owns, is endowed with or demonstrates.

Third, the lexicon presented above encompasses a wide range of acts that an authority figure may perform. No single word can provide sufficient definition of what we call leadership. Each word singles out one aspect of the complex business of managing or leading.

Fourth, the fact that a person assumes a position of leadership does not necessarily mean that he or she actually leads. A person becomes a leader only when he / she actually leads, neither before nor after.

Fifth, the lexicon provides an inventory of leadership functions: supervising, monitoring, censoring, deliberating, commanding, directing, overseeing, conserving, implementing, dispensing, driving, disciplining and more. Different words stress different functions. Closer scrutiny of the words prevailing in a given culture reveals the theoretical bias about leadership in that culture.

Sixth, values are embedded in the terms we use. Implicit in the term leader is a value judgment: for most people, it is preferable to be a leader than a follower. Furthermore, the word leader has acquired more prestige than the word manager or administrator.

Seventh, names of leadership positions in different cultures provide a glimpse into the roles the holders of such positions are expected to fulfill. For example, in America or Britain the term "mayor" is used for the chief executive of a municipality. The French transliterates the same term into *maire*. In a Palestinian village, the mayor is called *Mukhtār*, or the chosen one. The Egyptians prefer the term *ūmdeh*, a derivative of *amūd*, (or pillar). Egyptians also use *ameed*, a variation of the same root for dean of a college or head of a tribe. Palestinian term for mayor implies that the leader is one chosen by the constituency whereas the term used in Egypt stresses the fact that a leader is a person the constituency can depend on.

In conclusion, we should not be locked up in the word. As semanticists say, the word is not the thing. Instead we should focus on the activities that a position holder is expected to perform, how he or she actually performs, and the outcome of his or her performance. It is immaterial whether we call the person leader, administrator, manager, executive, or simply boss. In the final analysis what matters is what a person actually does, is expected to do or should be doing. It is the acts that matter.

Leadership Names and Titles in Different Languages

FIELDS	NAMES & TITLES
Military	Field Marshall, Marshall; Admiral; General, Colonel, Captain; Sergeant, Corporal, Commander. *Kaïd* or *Amir* (Arabic); Commissioner (of police)
Government	**Government**: Emperor, Czar, King or Queen; Regent; Raja (Malay for king or queen); Chancellor (chief minister of a state or chief secretary of a king); Sultan; President; Ruler. *Wali* (Arabic & Turkish for subordinate ruler); PM; DPM; Chancellor, Führer; Minister; Governor; Ra'is (Arabic for "head"); Chinese use characters symbolizing head **Malaysia**: Mentri-besar (Chief Minister in Malay); City Mayor **Palestine**: Mokhtar (the chosen one) city or village mayor **Egypt**: Mayor is called Omdeh, or pillar; governor of a city is called mohafez (conserver or protector) **Soviet Russia**: just "Comrade" **Persian**: Satrap, a governor of a province in ancient Persia or a subordinate ruler
Business	**Chairman**: CEO; COO, President **Managers**: Executive; Managing Director (or just Manager) Chief; Section (or Department) Head; SVP (or Just VP); Line or Staff Manager; Supervisor, entrepreneur; etc.
Education	**University**: Chancellor, Vice Chancellor; President; Provost **College**: Dean; Chairperson; Professor; Emeritus; etc. **Schools**: Principal, Headmaster; Mentor

Religion	Prophet, apostle, messenger (Arabic: *rasūll* or *nabi*), Pope or Pontiff, Cardinal, Bishop, etc.; Priest or Minister; (Arabic: *Imam* or *Sheikh*), not to mention hierarchy in other major religions and sects.
Politics	Speaker of the House; Party Leader; Majority or Minority Leader; Whip; Politician
Medical	Medical Director (and more recently Hospital Administrator); Surgeon, Matron; Head Nurse
Family	Father; mother; grandfather; Godfather; clan chief; tribe chief; older brother; older sister
General	Ra'i (Arabic for shepherd) vs. Ra'iyat (Arabic for subjects or people)

The names in the table above are labels of positions in various institutions or countries. Position holders are assigned the task of managing resources, organizing activities, administering, ruling or governing. In short, position holders lead people according to norms or laws of the social entities within which they operate. The labels are contrived and could very well be replaced by other labels to suit the tastes and ethos of the time.

QUALITIES FOLLOWERS EXPECT IN A LEADER
Empirical Study of Two Cultures

1. Methodology

Common conceptions of leadership represent various ideological and theoretical biases. Such conceptions are often thrust on managers by academicians or consultants, who are not directly involved in management. In this study, we reversed this tradition. We turned to the managers to learn from their experience as they try to meet the demands of two different classes of people, their superiors and their subordinates. Patterns of behavior, attitudes, thoughts and feelings depend on whether a person is dealing with a boss or with a subordinate. I do not see how we can talk about leadership without taking into consideration the person's actual position in relation to another in non-symmetrical power relation. In my seminars I advise participants to suspend the knowledge they accumulated over the years from their readings or training and consult their own experience. I simply ask them to answer two questions: What characterizes a boss that they like to work with. Similarly, what are those that characterize the kind of person whom they like to have as subordinate. The discussions that ensued are usually very rich and exciting. Participants soon realize how simplistic most criteria of effective leadership were. They begin to think about leadership at a concrete level and discover their prior assumptions. The most interesting outcome for me personally is the realization that what people learn about leadership is severed from their own experience.

Having achieved this insight I decided to use the same questions in formal research projects. The first thing I did was to standardize the format of the two questions and offer them to participants in a written form. One question pertains to qualities of the preferred boss and the other to those of the preferred subordinate. In this chapter I will deal only with the former. The actual question appears below.

"What are the THREE most important qualities that you require in a person that you would consider the BEST BOSS to work for? Please try to be as specific as possible and write only one distinct quality on each line below."

I conducted this study in two countries: Singapore and Malaysia. The Singaporean sample (457) was drawn from the private and public sectors. The Malaysian sample (260) was drawn from government ministries and semi-private agencies. Both samples are highly diversified groups of professionals who occupied top or middle management positions in their respective organizations. The method consisted of two written questions each followed by three numbered spaces. The numbered spaces were intended to encourage participants to specify rather than indulge in writing paragraphs. That would make the task of computation quite difficult.

My objective has been to formulate normative criteria of leadership that is empirically derived and, more importantly, based on the subjective experience of people immersed in management day after day. Using samples from Malaysia and Singapore was not meant to study cultural differences, something that could not be adequately met on the basis of responses to two questions. Rather it was done to see to what extent the same model would be applicable.

I invite the reader to respond to the same question and record the answer to compare later to the results of this survey. Thus, the reader will have the opportunity to share the same experience with the participants in the study and the benfit of comparing his thoughts and attitudes with them.

Compiling the Responses

I started by compiling a list of the responses provided by each of the groups surveyed. Each list was carefully inspected with the purpose of arriving at a classification system. The first inspection showed that the responses could be grouped in many different ways. I finally settled for the current classification into six major categories. Fortunately, the same system could be applied to both samples. The categories are briefly defined below. Table 1 shows the six categories in alphabetical order together with the frequency and percentage for both samples.

TABLE 1

Distribution of Major Categories of the Qualities of the Best Boss According to Singaporean Managers (N = 457) and Malaysian Managers (N = 260)

MAJOR CATEGORIES	FREQUENCY		PERCENTAGE	
	Singapore	Malaysia	Singapore	Malaysia
A. Character Traits	239	233	17%	27%
B. Communication	189	154	13%	18%
C. Moral Integrity	224	126	16%	15%
D. Leading	373	144	26%	17%
E. Mental Qualities	217	125	15%	14%
F. Supportive	183	88	13%	10%
TOTAL	1425	870	100%	101%

2. First Order Classification

Character qualities: I included in this category any response that identifies a positive feature in the character of the boss as a person irrespective of his / her role (or position) as a formal leader.

Communication: Qualities assigned to this category refer to the boss' ability or / and willingness to share information with subordinates.

Integrity: I included in this category responses that refer to morality or ethics.

Leading: This category covers a wide range of attributes pertaining to the boss in his / her formal position as a leader. This turned out to be a highly differentiated field. It reflects the diversity of views regarding what constitutes an effective leader.

Mental qualities. I included in this category any response that refers to the cognitive or intellectual performance of the boss.

Supportive attitude: This category refers to affective features of the preferred boss. It includes humanistic feelings such as sympathy, compassion, sensitivity, or behavior tendencies such as caring, helping or encouraging.

The fact that the categories are separate does not imply that they are unrelated features psychologically speaking. The separation is an artificial measure to group hundreds, and sometimes thousands, of items in a way that allow us to make sense out of them and make discoveries about the nature of superior–subordinate relationship that otherwise would remain hidden. Naturally, the data allows multiple classification systems. The choice depends on the judgment of the researcher in the light of his or her needs.

Interpretation of Statistical Findings

Let us start from the values in the bottom row which show that Singaporean managers reported 1,425 responses (3.1 responses per person). The Malaysian managers reported 870 responses (3.4 responses per person). The difference is due to the fact that more Singaporean than Malaysian managers participated in this study. The average is quite similar but exceeded slightly the rule of limiting the number of qualities to three. Focusing our attention on the last two columns, we will notice that *Leading* turned out to be the feature most widely endorsed by Singaporeans, accounting for 26 percent of the entire pool of qualities. *Character Qualities* came up as a remote second with 17 percent.

The ratio *Leading: Character Qualities* is reversed in the case of the Malaysians: *Character Qualities* (27 percent) exceed *Leading* by 16 percent.

It would appear that when you ask Singaporeans to assess the boss of their choice, their mind goes first to the boss's performance as a leader. In contrast, the Malaysians seem more concerned with the character qualities of the boss, while all other qualities — *leading* included — form a supportive or auxiliary background. In other words, Singaporeans seem to put more emphasis on the formal aspects. In contrast, the personal aspects dominate the formal in the case of the Malaysian managers.

This finding may suggest a cultural difference in the model of leadership that prevails in both countries. However, the data is merely suggestive and should not be considered conclusive at this point. However, it is perfectly legitimate to speculate freely without being conclusive. This finding is consistent with the custom prevalent both in Malaysia and Indonesia of addressing the boss by the endearing word "pak" or father. I am reminded of an incident in Malaysia. Malaysians used to use that term in addressing the Deputy Prime Minister. However, after he took over the premiership, people continued to address him the same way. One day, an official asked people to refrain from calling him "pak" on the grounds that "it is not polite anymore".

The statistical table shows a recurring feature. Statistical tables which I obtained from other samples show dominance of one feature with another feature, and sometimes two, as a second while the rest of the values are more or less low and equal. This may suggest that for a boss to be credible in the eyes of subordinates one feature at least must be prominent enough to act as anchor while many others are required as supportive background. Which feature is the most important and which will be auxiliary depends on the individual and cultural background of the subordinates.

3. Second Order Classification

The primary classification had the advantage of being convenient and easy to interpret. It accounted for every response. In other words, no response was left out. However, this advantage may give the illusion that the items included within each category are homogenous. They are of course if you look from a distance, but a closer look may reveal a lot of differences within each category. Therefore a second order classification is called for. Fortunately, it soon became clear that the items in all categories with the exception of the last category, "Supportive" are differentiated enough to justify second order classification. This process engendered 24 subcategories.

Any quality had to be included only in one subcategory. Often, a respondent would include more than one quality in a single response. When this occurred each quality was assigned to a different category, or to the same category as additional response. For example, the following responses

  a. **Character Qualities**
    1. Achievement-Oriented / Dedicated

    2. Assertive / Firm / Strong

    3. Courteous / Considerate / Tactful

    4. Energetic / Enthusiastic

    5. Mature / Stable / Secure

    6. Religious / Spiritual

    7. Sociable / Trusting

b. **Communication**

    8. Clear / Effective Communicator

    9. Expressive / Informative

    10. Receptive / Inquiring

c. **Integrity**

    11. Accountable / Responsible

    12. Fair / Impartial

    13. Honest / Sincere / Trustworthy

d. **Leading**

    14. Exercising Authority

    15. Boundary Spanning

    16. Delegating / Consulting

    17. Developing / Coaching

    18. Recognizing / Appreciating

e. **Mental Efficacy**

    19. Expertise / Technical Competence

    20. Innovative / Change Agent

    21. Intelligent

    22. Visionary / Strategic / Global

    23. Objective / Rational

f. **Supportive**

    24. Caring / Humanistic / Sympathetic

In the following section, we will go over these qualities one at a time. Subcategories will be also presented in alphabetical order within their respective categories. Each category will be referred to by multiple labels for the sake of clarity. The reason is that a single label can hardly reflect the complexity inherent in any human attribute.

I will give definitions of sub-categories, one at a time followed by examples of actual responses given by Singaporean and Malaysian subjects. More comprehensive lists of the responses of different Singaporean and Malaysian groups combined appear in Appendix II.

Character Qualities

This category includes seven sub-categories:

1. **Achievement-oriented / Hardworking / Dedicated**
   I included in this category any response that refers to the work ethics of the preferred leader — his / her motivation to achieve and succeed. Qualities such as effectiveness, efficiency, hard work, goal attainment and task orientation were also included.

2. **Assertive / Strong**
   This category covers responses that stress aggressiveness, competitiveness, or readiness to confront. This sub-category complements the previous cluster in that it determines the style a boss adopts in his or her achievement striving.

3. **Courteous / Tactful / Considerate**
   This sub-category came to my attention in a previous research.

4. **Energetic / Enthusiastic**
   The common denominator of the attributes covered by this sub-category is the emphasis on the dynamism of the boss. The themes in this cluster of traits appear similar to the themes covered by the second category (number 2). Both stress the outward manifestation of energy. There is, however, a significant difference that warrants separating both sets of attributes: here the responses imply that energy is channeled towards a desirable outcome colored by optimism and excitement. But in the former trait of assertiveness energy is directed *against* an obstacle accompanied by hostility or aggressiveness. The difference is essentially temperamental.

5. **Mature / Stable**
   The emphasis here is on the leader's mental health and personality integration. Responses in this group include such traits as the ability to withstand stress; sound judgment; wisdom; or capacity to recover quickly from emotional upset.

6. **Religious / Spiritual**
   This is self-explanatory. This feature did not occur at all in the list provided by Singaporean respondents and occurred rarely in the data provided by their Malaysian counterparts.

7. **Sociable / Trusting**

I included in this sub category characteristics that belong to the well-known personality trait of Extraversion.

Table 2 displays the frequencies and percentages of the seven themes for both Singaporean and Malaysian managers. Let us start by the values in the bottom row.

The Singaporean and Malaysian groups reported a total of 239 and 233 character qualities consecutively. The first two columns display the relative frequencies of each of the 7 themes for both groups independently. The last two columns display the corresponding percentages. The latter should form the basis for interpretation.

TABLE 2
Character Qualities attributed to the preferred boss by
Singaporean Managers (N = 457) and Malaysian Managers (N = 260)

MAJOR CATEGORIES	FREQUENCY		PERCENTAGE	
	Singapore	Malaysia	Singapore	Malaysia
1. Achievement Drive	43	63	18%	27%
2. Assertive / Strong	23	21	10%	09%
3. Courteous / Tactful	105	60	44%	26%
4. Energetic / Enthusiastic	10	05	04%	02%
5. Mature / Stable	43	37	18%	16%
6. Religious / Spiritual	0	9	00%	04%
7. Sociable / Trusting	15	38	06%	16%
TOTAL	239	233	100%	100%

Some striking features emerge from Table 2:

First, "Courteous / Tactful" emerged as the leading theme in the Singaporean responses (44%). "Achievement" and "Mature" came in second place but lagged far behind. The three themes combined account for 80% of the attributes provided by Singaporeans. The same three themes dominate the list of Malaysians as well, accounting for 69% of their responses. However, while courtesy came out far ahead of all the other themes, courtesy and achievement were almost equal in the Malaysian responses and moderately more frequent than the other themes. What is most striking in this table is the salience of courtesy in the overall character profile of the boss according to both cultural groups, statistical differences notwithstanding.

Second, equally striking is the absence (or near absence) of religion in the reported qualities in both groups. This is interesting in view of the fact that religion is known to have played a dominant role in the Malay culture and seems to be rising significantly in Singaporean society in recent years.

Third, sociability as a desirable trait in the character profile of the boss is stressed more frequently by Malaysians than Singaporeans (16% and 6% consecutively).

To conclude:

Singaporean and Malaysian managers look up to a boss who is primarily civil in his / her manners, respectful of subordinates, dedicated and hardworking, and emotionally stable and mature. Such are the most frequently reported prerequisites of a boss.

Communication Qualities

Communication Category (Table 3) encompasses three components: Clarity or Effective communication, Expressiveness or Transmitting and Receiving or Soliciting of information.

TABLE 3
COMMUNICATION QUALITIES
Frequencies and Percentages of Sub-Categories Provided by
Singaporean Managers (N = 457) and Malaysian Managers (N = 260)

MAJOR CATEGORIES	FREQUENCY		PERCENTAGE	
	Singapore	Malaysia	Singapore	Malaysia
8. Clarity / Effectiveness	70	11	37.0 %	7.0%
9. Expressive / Transmitting	22	22	12.0 %	14.0%
10. Receiving / Soliciting	97	121	51.0%	79.0%
TOTAL	189	154	100.0%	100.0%

8. **Clarity**

   Responses included in this category cover a wide range of content that the preferred boss expressed — goals, visions, roles, objectives, or mission. In many responses, the reference was to the boss's thinking. It would have been appropriate to have included these responses in category E "Mental Efficacy". I finally decided to include it in the communication category. The reason is that when, for example person A attributes clarity to another person B, the implication is that B has been able to make himself understood clearly by A. It follows that clarity in this sense qualifies the communication process. Only by inference can A impute clarity to the thought process of B.

In other words, clarity in communication describes a message that has been successfully transmitted from one person to another. It follows that clarity is essentially an interpersonal phenomenon. Meanwhile, clarity can be an attribute of a person's thinking in which case it would be a purely subjective experience that other people may or may not detect.

9. **Expressing / Transmitting**

Communication can be either outgoing or incoming; expressing or internalizing, exporting or importing. Specifying whether communication is one or the other, I thought would be of considerable diagnostic value. Some of the attributes describes communicated messages and could, therefore, be included in the subcategory "Expressing / Transmitting".

10. **Receiving / Soliciting**

Responses in this subcategory put the accent on the receptive aspect of communication.

Table 3 shows the distribution of the three aspects of communication for Singaporean and Malaysians. The most significant finding is that Receptivity exceeds that of Transmitting in both groups. That is to say a boss is appreciated to the extent that he or she is receptive to messages from subordinates, appreciates and accepts suggestions from them and is willing to receive feedback or solicit information from them. The ratio "receiving : giving information" can be valuable as a diagnostic index.

Moral Integrity

(See Table 4.)

TABLE 4
COMPONENTS OF MORAL INTEGRITY
Qualities of Moral Integrity attributed to the preferred boss by
Singaporean Managers (N = 457) and Malaysian Managers (N = 260)

MAJOR CATEGORIES	FREQUENCY		PERCENTAGE	
	Singapore	Malaysia	Singapore	Malaysia
11. Accountable	28	45	13%	35%
12. Fair / Equitable	96	44	43%	34%
13. Honest / Sincere	100	39	45%	31%
TOTAL	224	128	101%	100%

11. **Accountable / Responsible**

This theme focuses on the leader living up to his commitment.

12. **Fair / Equitable**

This is self-evident.

13. **Honest / Sincere**

Leadership Qualities

(See Table 5.) Leading category turned out to be very complex. As shown in Table 5, Leading comprises five distinct components (nos. 14 through 18). I shall define briefly each one of these components. Starting with no. 14, exercise of authority or will to lead we noted that even at this level, the sub-category appears to be very complex. We cannot therefore define clearly unless we break it down into four clusters of traits starting with the responses that refer to overall control:

a. Readiness to take charge

b. Decisiveness

c. Personal Influence / Role Model

The latter cluster is indicated by such responses as "gains respect by performance not by command", "leads by example", "motivates", "able to inspire people", "motivates rather than give orders", "charismatic", "inspirational", "able to evoke enthusiasm", "able to inspire and lead effectively", "encourages subordinates to channel their creative energies", "able to get the best out of subordinates", "good example to others", "good example to emulate".

d. Organizational ability or managerial proficiency

15. **Boundary Management**

Two distinct clusters of traits could be discerned in this sub-category. First, across boundary activities — included in this cluster are responses indicating that the leader's influence extends beyond his or her immediate subordinates. In other words, the leader acts not only as a boss of a group of subordinates, but also as a representative of the group vis-à-vis other groups and the organization as a whole. Furthermore, he engages in public relations activities in the service of the group. Second, boundary protection — responses in this cluster refer to the leader's tendency to defend the group from outside interference or disruption.

16. **Delegating / Sharing Power**

17. **Developer**

18. **Recognition**

Table 5 provides an excellent profile of a model boss according to both the Singaporean and the Malaysian managers. The most widely appreciated feature is "exercise of authority".

TABLE 5

COMPONENTS OF LEADERSHIP CATEGORY

Leadership Qualities Attributed to the Preferred Boss by
Singaporean Managers (N = 457) & Malaysian Managers (N = 260)

MAJOR CATEGORIES	FREQUENCY		PERCENTAGE	
	Singapore	Malaysia	Singapore	Malaysia
14. Exercises Authority	234	89	63	62
15. Boundary Spanning	21	3	6	2
16. Delegating / Consulting	51	18	14	13
17. Developing	26	13	7	9
18. Recognition	41	21	11	15
TOTAL	373	144	101	101

The Singaporean group provided 373 attributes pertaining to the major category of leading. Of these 234 or 63% belong to subcategory 14 "Exercise of Authority". Corresponding value obtained by Malaysian managers is very close (62%).

Mental Qualities

(See Table 6.)

TABLE 6
MENTAL QUALITIES
Components of Mental Qualities Attributed to the Preferred Boss by
Singaporean Managers (N = 457) & Malaysian Managers (N = 260)

MAJOR CATEGORIES	FREQUENCY		PERCENTAGE	
	Singapore	Malaysia	Singapore	Malaysia
19. Expertise	111	46	51%	37%
20. Innovative	09	33	04%	26%
21. Intelligent	06	11	03%	09%
22. Visionary	58	29	27%	23%
23. Objective / Rational	33	06	15%	05%
Total	217	125	100%	100%

19–23. Expertise / Professional competence / Innovative visionary: Includes foresight and contextual thinking

When it comes to the mental aspects, expertise and visionary outlook stand out for both groups. More Malaysians than Singaporeans endorsed the innovativeness — 26% compared to only 4% reported by the Singaporeans.

4. General Discussion

We start out from the premise that contradiction is inherent in the manager's role — managers have to shift back and forth between leading their subordinates and following their immediate superiors, not to mention having to respond to demands of several peers over whom they have no power. Three findings are worth stressing:

First, the emergence of the concept of boundary management. One of the most valuable insights I got from this survey and other surveys that I had conducted in the US is that workers admire a boss who establishes presence beyond the boundary of the group. Participants, at least some of them, are not fully satisfied with the leader that confines his attention to internal concerns of the group. They expect the leader to represent the group in its dealings with others. The outside systems which the boss has to deal with on behalf of the group is not a clearly defined constituency. Dealing with an outside system is a completely different ball game. The outside world is incoherent, ambiguous and unpredictable. Furthermore, the leader has no authority over most of the external systems. Therefore, the leader must rely heavily on his personal resources and the backing he may or my not get from his own leadership. That calls for different set of requirements: tolerance of ambiguity, ability to deal with uncertainty, and negotiation skill.

It seems that there is more to the managerial role than simply providing local leadership. Subjects in the study ascribe an external dimension to the managerial role and that it is the responsibility of the manager to link his or her work group to other groups in the organization and to the organization as a whole.

Subjects also believe that leaders who exercise influence outside their units are likely to gain more power and more credibility among their charges than managers who immerse themselves totally in their units' internal affairs. Such "boundary spanning" managers facilitate functional exchange with other units and external groups and foster their subordinates' identification with the organization as a whole.

Second, conspicuous absence of references to intelligence: It is interesting that intelligence is conspicuously absent from the list of qualities that our subjects expect in a boss. It seems that what managers expect from a leader is more "the fruits" of his or her intelligence rather than intelligence in itself. That is probably why they stressed such attributes as: clarity, sound judgment, coherence in decision making and ingenuity in solving technical problems they encounter. Even the quality they call "clarity" is not associated in their minds with unusual, sophisticated thinking but rather with the leader's ability "to grasp the totality of a given situation" and "to be able to see future possibilities". Similarly, when respondents talk about "vision" they do not refer to exceptional creative ability but to ordinary foresight tempered by common sense and the ability to grasp things as they are.

Third, leaders come in many forms with varied styles and diverse qualities. One ideal model would be too restricting. It would deny diversity. Effective leaders are extraordinarily diverse both in their personal attributes and leadership styles.

5. Broader Implications

The survey enables us to sketch the portraits of exemplary leaders. In fact it offers us several types of portraits. What we got here is an inventory of attributes that characterize leaders that people aspire to have. No one person can possess all these attributes. But different sets of attributes are realized by different leaders. I see the list as a diagnostic assessment instrument. If I want to articulate the reasons why I admire one leader but not another, I just seek an answer through the list. In fact I am much better able now to assess a leader's performance than I have ever been before I compiled this inventory. The reader may go through the list of attributes to find out which among them characterize the leader of his / her choice. The reader may try one more exercise — identify which attributes characterize him or her as a boss and which are missing or irrelevant.

As you spell out the attributes of the leader that you admire (and like to associate yourself with), you are simultaneously expressing your own personal needs. You may also be expressing what you miss in your current boss. From this we may look at the distribution of the different categories of attributes as a hierarchy of needs in a given culture. Boss-subordinate relationship is wrongly called business or formal relationship. In fact it is a very intimate relationship. It reaches deeply into one's consciousness and affects one's quality of life and sense of identity. After all career salience in one's life is an established reality. One's career depends to a great extent on one's relationship with the immediate boss. Let us not forget that workers typically spend more time with their bosses than with their spouses or close relatives. Mobility between jobs tempers that effect. A favorable superior-subordinate relationship contributes to job satisfaction or mitigates job dissatisfaction.

Why did I ask participants in the study to think of three attributes? I could have requested the most important single attribute. I thought that would be too artificial. It seems arbitrary to describe another person, or oneself, in terms of a single characteristic. People are not that simple. Furthermore, it is inconceivable that anyone would admire another person for a single reason. I thought three attributes would provide an optimally differentiated profile of the perceived model leader. Thus the list of attributes can serve as "menu" or inventory that should be helpful in identifying the characteristics that distinguish between leaders.

Fields of Leadership Action

It was once believed that if leadership traits were truly present in an individual they would manifest themselves almost without regard to the situation in which the person was functioning. No one believes that any more. Acts of leadership take place in an unimaginable variety of settings, and the setting does much to determine the kinds of leader that emerge and how they play their roles.

— John W. Gardner[7]

Contextual Thinking

Leadership is often seen as an intrapersonal phenomenon that originates in an individual. According to this view influence flows in one direction, namely from the leader to other individuals or to a group of individuals. This conception fails to reflect the complexity of the phenomenon. No one can quarrel with the fact that leadership is activity undertaken by individuals. However, what is often forgotten or deliberately ignored is that leaders emerge in social settings and exercise leadership in fields whose dynamic forces impact the leader and determine the ultimate outcome of his or her efforts. These fields are very different from each other. Furthermore, the leader's influence may target single individuals, structured groups or groups striving to

---

[7] Gardner, J. W. (1986). Leadership Papers/ 1 "The Mature Leadership". Washington, DC: Independent Sector.

get structured, an aggregate of interdependent groups, corporations, city states or multinational corporations. All these fields may be called organizations. But in the final analysis they are all social systems. It follows that a leader must be conceptually oriented to the properties and dynamics of the setting where he sets out to lead. This requires understanding of the properties of the field and readiness to shift perspective as the leader moves from one field to another.

The starting point for us should be the recognition that even though leadership refers to individual actions, yet they are actions of individuals involved in public life. No matter how introverted a leader may be, he or she is involved in public life. The second point is that leadership is an integral feature of any social system. As such it could not be understood in isolation from the social system that gives rise to it. We cannot conceptualize one without the other. Third point is that leadership is the exercise of influence on a social *system*, not on isolated individuals. Even in the case of leading an individual, that individual is in reality a whole universe. He or she is not only embedded in a culture but also carries the culture within him or her. He or she moves in the world as the center of a network of relationships invisible as they may be to others. A purely intrapersonal approach to leadership is therefore futile.

Formal Organizations

It follows that the first task of any leader is to conceptualize the social system where he or she is supposed to perform. Mapping the field and understanding its dynamics is a prerequisite of effective leadership. So let us start by understanding what we mean by organization. I think the safest way to start would be by consulting the dictionary. The dictionary gives us the following meanings[8]:

❖ An organization is *something that is organized* such as an organic structure; composition or a group of persons organized for some end or work, the functionaries of a political party along with the offices, committees, etc., that they fill.

❖ The state or manner of *being organized.*

---

[8] Random House Webster.

❖ The act or *process of organizing* or pertaining to an organization.

The first two meanings refer to *something*, a finite and distinguishable entity that exists somewhere and that this something consists of components — individuals or groups — that work together in an *organized* fashion. The third meaning refers to the *act* or *process* of organizing. What the dictionary does not explicitly indicate is the relationship that exists between this *something* and the *process* of organizing.

Thinking simultaneously of the word "organization" and its antonyms gives us a better grasp of the dynamic nature of any organization. This point needs to be stressed because of the prevalent conception of the organization as *something* that stands out there against the environment as a background. Students of management scarcely imagine the organization as a process and that the *something* is in reality ongoing processes of organizing and that the concept of leadership refers to people who do the organizing. It follows that the primary requirement of leadership is to understand what they are supposed to organize and what kind of organization they want to structure and how to maintain that structure.

Organization as Emerging Entity

The organization is often conceived as a container *inside* of which people work. This conception reflects concrete thinking so prevalent among bureaucrats whose daily work is within a building with minimum of contact with or lack of imagination of what goes on outside the "headquarters". I call that the "headquarters illusion". Unfortunately, the emphasis on the luxury of the headquarters and its image enhances the power of this illusion over the minds of employees. The building is just the rallying place where we gather but our work consists of transactions with many people in the building or outside. It follows that the organization is a communication system. Through communication we conduct our business.

An organization comes into being through deliberate efforts of enterprising individuals. Such individuals decide *to take charge* of available resources and exploit them further *in a given field*. However, no organization can survive or grow by efforts of single individuals.

Individuals must transcend their individualities to structure a collectivity that interfaces with the world as a whole entity. An organization may be a firm, an army, a school or a bank. It may be a private or public institution. It may be a kinship system such as a family or tribe, a civil society or a special interest group. It may be a transitory committee or a project team with short time frame.

We are all too familiar with organizations that are fully developed entities while the concept of the organization as a process fades by comparison. The organization is not, and could not be a *finished* entity. It is always in a state of flux: it grows, expands, declines, recovers, matures and may ultimately dissolve. And when an organization breaks up, it vanishes leaving no trace behind. But its former members do not vanish, they simply disperse. Survival is not guaranteed, randomness is inevitable, rules and procedures are only ideas on paper or in the minds of individuals. Rules become real only when they are acted out. And they are acted out only when monitored by people in charge. It does not matter much what we call people in charge. We may call them managers, leaders, supervisors, or administrators. It is apt to think of the organization as a *project* in constant emergence rather than as a static entity that springs into existence in one act. It is also prudent to see it as a historical entity with uncertain life span. In the course of its life span, the organization continues to strive in its environment.

With this in mind, leadership may be understood as aggregate of activities of many members of the organization. Leadership therefore is primarily a societal phenomenon. It is a drama acted out in many theatres and according to many different scenarios. Furthermore, the organization is not an opaque entity or undifferentiated mass of people. In conclusion, the willful act of *organizing* is the very essence of leadership. This means that the intrapersonal approach to leadership cannot tell us the whole story of leadership. We will have to place leadership in a social context.

Inevitability of Disorder

We can better understand organizing processes by contrasting them with the opposite processes. With this in mind, let us go back to the dictionary to look up the antonyms of the word organization. There we will find two sets of verbs, implying actions or processes:

❖ Dissolve, disband, dismember, or break up

❖ Disorganize, throw into confusion or disorder

Organizing processes constitute half the story of any social system. Forces of disorganization will always be at work. The opposing processes coexist at both the organic and societal levels of existence. The fact that an organization is called organization does not necessarily mean that it is optimally organized, or that it will always be able to sustain current levels of organization. Forces of growth and decay coexist in any living system. An organized state is nothing other than a state of dynamic equilibrium, a balance between opposing forces of order and disorder.

Organization at a societal level is too complex to grasp without guidance from the knowledge we derive from simpler forms of life, namely organisms. Organisms survive and grow by balancing the opposing forces of *anabolism* and *catabolism*. Anabolism is the constructive metabolism, the synthesis of more complex substances from simpler ones. It is opposed by *catabolism*, the destructive metabolism; the breaking down in living organisms of more complex substances into simpler ones, with the release of energy. The dictionary is not enough. So writers resort to analogies. The closest and most popular is the organism. Bertrand Russell, a philosopher mathematician notes[9]

> … the biology of organizations depends upon the fact that an organisation is also an organism, with a life of its own, and a tendency to growth and decay. Competition between organizations is analogous to competition between individual animals and plants, and can be viewed in a more or less Darwinian manner. But this analogy, like others, must not be pressed too far; it may serve to suggest and to illuminate, but not to demonstrate. For example, we must not assume that decay is inevitable where social organisations are concerned. (p. 107)

Interestingly, the same analogy, with the same reservations, was used by a statesman, Woodrow Wilson:

---

[9] Russell, B. (1985). *Power: A New Social Analysis*, London: Unwin Paperbacks (first published 1938).

The trouble with the [Newtonian] theory is that the
government is not a machine but a living thing. It falls,
not under the theory of universe, but under the theory of
organic life. It is accountable to Darwin, not to Newton.
It is modified by its environment, necessitated by its tasks,
shaped to its functions by the sheer pressure of life. No living
thing can have its organs offset against each other as checks
and live. On the contrary, its life is dependent upon their
quick cooperation, their ready response to the commands of
instinct or intelligence, their amicable community of purpose.
Government is not a body of blind forces; it is a body of men,
with highly differentiated functions, no doubt...but with a
common task.... Their cooperation is indispensable.... This is
not theory, but fact, and displays its force as fact, whatever may
be thrown across its track. Living political constitutions must
be Darwinian in structure and practice.[10]

However, a distinction must be made between life and non-life as
Asinov (1972) explains:

A living organism can, however, "make the effort" of decreas-
ing the entropy of at least part of the system in which it is
involved (at the expense, admittedly, of increasing the entropy
of the rest of the system still more). Even the simplest moving
organism can enforce a local decrease in entropy by jumping,
flying, climbing, walking, crawling, or swimming upward. Even
sessile[11] organisms such as an oyster can enforce local decrease
in entropy in various fashions other than bodily movement.
(p. 61)

In the final analysis organizing is nothing other than the deliberate
effort we exert in trying to manage available energies, whether those
that are inherent in people or locked up in natural resources. Perfect
equilibrium is impossible to reach. The best we can hope for is
maintaining an optimum level of equilibrium as long as we can. In
organic forms of life, this takes place in a natural way. The organism
is equipped to do that. But human organizations are not natural. They

---

[10] Quoted by Tulis, 1987, p. 121.
[11] Botany, attached directly at the base: sessile leaves.

are social artifacts, contrived, or invented. The process of maintaining optimal equilibrium has to be deliberate. This makes the organization an end product or an output. We are more used to the notion that the organization is a source of output and origin of activities.

The Law of Entropy

Since energy is our vital resource, we may benefit from thermodynamics,[12] the study of a primary source of energy, namely heat. The fundamental law of thermodynamics concerns the conservation of energy. According to this law only a certain fraction of heat energy could be converted to work, and no more, even under ideal conditions; that is, even if friction were to be eliminated and no energy were to be lost to the outside world. The second law of thermodynamics is what concerns us here. It is called the law of *Entropy*. Entropy of the system is defined as "the amount of energy lost to the system, or the amount of energy not available to work by the system". The second law further stipulates that "any system if left to itself, meaning without exchange with the external environment, entropy will inevitably increase".

It must be stated that entropy is a relative notion. It implies loss of energy (or increased randomness) pertaining to a given system. The energy lost to one system may be a gain to another system. I must stress here that energy in thermodynamics is stated as a measurable quantity. We cannot apply it literally to human systems but it can provide us with a healthy cognitive approach to the business of leading social systems. But organization level is not uniform. It varies from time to time and from one type of collectivity to another. Take, for example, a crowd in a busy square in a large city. A crowd consists of unrelated individuals who happened to be in close proximity at a given time. In a crowd, each individual is heading somewhere and pursues his own agenda. No common goal, no collective action, no interest in other people. In other words, there is no sense of community, there is no *membership*. Here we witness a high degree of randomness, or a low

---

[12] From the Greek words meaning the movement of heat.

degree of organization. Only when perceptions are shared, ideas are exchanged and common interests are realized does a group emerge. The degree of organization depends primarily on the volume and quality of interpersonal communication and the emergence of leadership. Time also is a very important factor to consider. Variability depends on the impact of internal and external events. We can never achieve a perfect state of equilibrium. The system is equally vulnerable as it approaches either end.[13] In fact, loose control under certain circumstances may be life-preserving. The downfall can come abruptly or gradually.

A large corporation is not necessarily less vulnerable than a tiny one. A full one-third of the Fortune 500 industries listed in 1970 had vanished by 1983. Today, the average lifetime of the largest industrial enterprises is probably less than half the average lifetime of a person in an industrial society. The geography we studied in school has become obsolescent. Many states that seemed eternal disappeared and new ones emerged. Empires dissolved themselves. Leaders need to understand, not only the factors enhancing survival, but also the forces of decay that are lurking in the system. Only an organization that is optimally organized has a chance of survival. A rigidly organized firm or department in government is unable to respond to varied environmental demands. It is unable to adapt to changes in its environment. An extremely disorganized firm does not function as a united entity. Every part will respond in its own way. Therefore it is incumbent on us to assess the level of organization and develop criteria for what we consider the optimum level of organization. The optimum will depend on the type of activity we will engage in. Different tasks require different levels of organization and different degrees of interdependence among the people that are required to undertake the tasks.

Perceived Level of Organization

But we need also to bear in mind that how organized or disorganized a situation is depends on the perceiver's state of mind. The same

---

[13] Many reputable organizations survive the same way as patients who are kept alive by various life-sustaining devices. When an organization is dissolved, it leaves no trace but former members continue to exist. When an old car stops functioning it becomes a burden on its owner, the owner would pay money for whoever can take it away.

situation may be judged by person A to be disorganized while B considers it sufficiently organized. As a result A feels disoriented in it while B is able to orient himself within it. We may infer that A is overly sensitive to disorder or intolerant of ambiguity. In contrast B is not so sensitive or intolerant. To the uninformed, a street brawl in Cairo appears random or even chaotic while those who live in Cairo find it perfectly predictable. In fact the events constituting the brawl follow a certain order and unfold according to unwritten script. The brawl usually ends up well but may go out of hand leading to tragic consequences. This is like the case of the tourist witnessing situations he or she cannot comprehend. The same problem plagues anthropologists who conduct studies in foreign cultures. Often they are baffled by the apparent bizarreness of events. They try to explain them from the standpoint of their own cultures.

Variations in perception of order has been recognized by Sun Tzu and even put to good use in tactical approaches to the enemy:

> Amid the turmoil and tumult of battle there may be seeming disorder and yet no real disorder at all; amid confusion and chaos, your array may be without head or tail yet it will be proof against defeat. Simulated disorder postulates perfect discipline; simulated fear postulates courage; simulated weakness postulates strength. Hiding order beneath the cloak of disorder is simply a question of subdivision; concealing courage under a show of timidity presupposes a fund of latent energy; masking strength with weakness is to be effected by tactical dispositions. (*The Art of War*, p. 22)

Managers are trained in the art of control. They were led to believe that any sign of disorder (or low level of organization) is evil that should be avoided at any cost. Heightened sensitivity to disorder has become an integral aspect of our educational philosophy. Much energy is expended in the direction of imposing order. On the other hand, perceived order may be a façade concealing forces of disintegration. This is the plight of dictatorial system that gives the dictator the illusion that law and order is well established. Often the apparent order may conceal dynamic forces of disorder the dictator is unable to detect or do not want to detect. Constructive and destructive forces go hand in hand.

Edward Hall (1977)[14], an American anthropologist refers to a news item he read in *The New York Times* about a campaign by U.S. Park Police to stamp out kite flying on the grounds of the Washington Monument. Hall noted that "Park Police charter to harass the kite fliers lay in an old law written by Congress supposedly to keep the Wright brothers' planes from becoming fouled in kite strings." Hall thinks that this incidence "bolsters the psychoanalyst Laing's conviction that Western world is mad." Hall adds the following critical remark about institutions in general:

> … it is not man who is crazy so much as his institutions and those culture patterns that determine his behavior. We in the West are alienated from ourselves and from nature. We labor under a number of delusions, one of which is that life makes sense; i.e., that we are sane. We persist in this view despite massive evidence to the contrary. We live fragmented, compartmentalized lives in which contradictions are carefully sealed off from each other. We have been taught to think linearly rather than comprehensively… (p. 11)

Hall goes on to point out that this feature reflects a culturally determined cognitive style characteristic of Western cultures:

> The delusional aspects have to do with the institutionalized necessity to control "everything," and the widely accepted notion that the bureaucrat knows what is best; never for a moment does he doubt the validity of the bureaucratic solution. It is also slightly insane, or at least indicative of our incapacity to order priorities with any common sense … and we do this not through conscious design or because we are not intelligent or capable but because of the way in which deep cultural undercurrents structure life in subtle but highly consistent ways that are not consciously formulated. Like the invisible jet streams in the skies that determine the course of a storm, these hidden currents shape our lives; yet their influence is only beginning to be identified. Given our linear, step-by-step, compartmentalized way of thinking, fostered by the schools and public media, it is impossible for our leaders to consider events

---

[14]Hall, E. T. (1977). *Beyond Culture*. Garden City, New York: Anchor Books / Doubleday.

comprehensively or to weigh priorities according to a system of common good, all of which can be placed like an unwanted waif on culture's doorstep. (pp. 11, 12)

Notion of Boundary

Life of an organism could not be contained within the body. It propels the organism in the space around it. The mind projects the individual beyond the present moment. Sensory perception is complemented by imagination. Imagination deals with possibilities that are not accessible to sense perception. We stressed that the livelihood of any system depends on its effectiveness of exchange with other systems in the environment. This means that the living system is inherently open. Autonomy means that the system is capable of maintaining itself as an independent entity but is secure enough to go beyond itself. In other words it exists as a force in the environment. The concept of boundary comes to mind. To maintain its presence in the environment as a force, the system must be able to manage its boundary in such a way as to maximize input-output exchange with other systems without losing its identity.

Boundary of a social system should not be interpreted as a static container or enclosure. Rather it should be seen as activities of exchange with other systems. Take the example of a cell in the organism. The cell membrane is the communication link between the cell and other cells. Or take the example of the senses. The senses receive, register, reach out, inform, thus allowing the organism to thrive as a *force* capable of orienting itself in the world beyond its skin. The analogy of the skin is apt. It is more than a container of the different organs of the body. It illustrates the dynamism of the boundary of any system. The skin has pores to let substances in and out in an orderly and dynamic fashion. It contains sweat glands that help maintain a constant body temperature. It is in the skin that the body manufactures vitamin D. The notion of boundary in this light is not geographic or spatial in a narrow sense. It is more than a circumference or demarcation area. It should be interpreted dynamically, that is as structured activities intended to allow the system to maintain its autonomy separate from other systems in an environment. This is the protective function. But the boundary performs functions of exchange.

In an organism, the process of exchange takes place spontaneously, triggered by mechanisms built into the organism. In social systems, boundary transactions (interdependence) have to be deliberately managed. Your primary responsibility as a manager is to oversee the interactions that should take place between your group and other groups, those within your organization or outside such as clients, suppliers, and many others. Naturally, a vigorous and alert system can keep the boundary somewhat closed, or open it as the need arises. To keep the boundary closed, a system (meaning people who are in charge) must take certain protective or defensive measures. Sometimes the system has to expand its boundary. That inevitably will cause the boundary of neighboring systems to contract. Thus, acquisition, invasion, empire building, annexation, spying, infiltrating, monitoring, represent challenges that have to be defined. At other times, the system may decide to contract its boundary. Thus we get divesting, giving away, or sharing. A third category of boundary activity is cooperative exchange or contractual agreement.

Janus

Janus, in Roman mythology, the god of doors and gateways, and also of beginnings. His principal temple in the Forum had doors facing east and west for the beginning and ending of the day, and between them stood his statue with two faces, gazing in opposite directions. In every home the morning prayer was addressed to him, and in every domestic undertaking his assistance was sought. As the god of beginnings, he was publicly invoked on the first day of January, the month that was named for him because it began the new year. He was involed too at the beginning of wars, during which the doors of his temple in the Forum always stood open; when Rome was at peace, the doors were closed. For the author of this book, Janus symbolizes the dual role of the leader at the boundary of the constituency (internal and external).

[Source: Encarta Reference Library 2004]

Organizing Processes

By the term *organize* I mean deliberate attempts of an individual (or group) to bring order and predictably to the system under his charge. I have in mind two global sets of efforts: integration and differentiation.

1. Integration Mechanisms

By integration we mean the effort geared towards getting the specialized subsystems to work together in a concerted fashion, thus maintaining the wholeness of the system. As differentiation increases, the system needs to divert more of its energy to integration efforts. Spontaneous biological integration takes place through a variety of mechanisms: blood circulation, digestive, circulatory and other vital subsystems, endocrine system, sympathetic and parasympathetic nervous system. The living organism provides us with a model of both integration and differentiation. Understandably, we will never be able to copy organic processes but we can be guided by them. In human organization four integration mechanisms could be identified:

Organization Mission

The mission defines the organization's reason for existence: the kind of business it engages in or the service it offers. The mission serves as a guide for designing and managing the development effort. It helps to determine the choice of strategic options. The mission should highlight what is unique about the organization relative to other organizations in the same field. It should provide a vision. A mission is, or should be, a realistic or rational mandate. It is different but not separate from a vision. A vision is a subjective image of the shape of things to be. A visionary leader is a leader who fires people's imagination and get them to see in their minds' eye future conditions that are far more pleasant than the current state of affairs. The mission helps to determine the choice of strategic options. A mission should ideally determine organizational strategies, objectives and policies. At least these should be consistent with the stated mission. Otherwise, the mission would be superfluous as it really is in some opportunistic organizations.

Cultural Values

A mission has to be justified by a set of values that serve as regulator of our activities. But what values? The values that help members of the organization make human sense out of the organization's efforts. Values are set of norms of conduct that guide our exchange processes with clients, the public, or personnel. Values include the organization's interpretation of the worth of the human person, social responsibility and responsibility towards the environment. Take the example of an investment bank. Management should be concerned with more than just controlling risks and choosing the right computer system. The most difficult task of all is to form a viable corporate culture. The culture is the mental and emotive context of our daily life. Values constitute a significant component of corporate culture. They allow people to rally around the mission. They must transcend individual interests and personal egotism. The mission is both descriptive and rational. It engages the human mind and helps people in an organization to integrate at a conceptual level. But people are not driven by ideas, they are driven by emotions.

Bertrand Russell (1985) expresses this in a concise form:

> Social cohesion demands a creed, or a code of behaviour, or a prevailing sentiment, or best, some combination of all three; without something of the kind, a community disintegrates, and becomes subject to a tyrant or a foreign conqueror. But if this

means of cohesion is to be effective, it must be very deeply felt; it may be imposed by force upon a small minority, provided they are not specially important through exceptional intelligence or character, but it must be genuine and spontaneous in the great majority. Loyalty to a leader, national pride, and religious fervor have proved, historically, the best means of securing cohesion; but loyalty to a leader is less permanently effective than it used to be, owing to the decay of hereditary sovereignty, and religious fervor is threatened by the spread of free thought.[15]

Leadership Hierarchy

Authority structure should be designed in such a way as to fulfill the function of both vertical and horizontal integration. That brings to mind the concept of core executive. The function of integration is assigned to a central authority, a leader or whoever represents the collectivity. However, a single individual cannot fulfill this function without creating conditions on the ground that facilitate the incumbent's task. A central leader is the locus of most decision making and an important transmission point of messages to different layers of the structured collectivity.[16]

Training Practices

Going back to the law of entropy, we note that one of the forces of deterioration is the inevitability of obsolescence. Monitoring obsolescence is a major task of leadership. Organization survival and growth are not possible without integrative learning strategy. Learning should be a daily concern and strategic issue at the same time. This would be only possible if supervision includes more than just getting the job done, namely assessment of current capabilities, and designing development programs. We should transcend the rigid tradition of

---

[15] Russell, B. (1985). *Power: A New Social Analysis*. London: Unwin Paperbacks (first published, 1938).

[16] Frankfort, H. (1948). *Ancient Egyptian Religion: An Interpretation*. New York: Harper & Row.

conventional seminars and workshops. Innovation is badly needed in the area of training.

Technology

Technology provides integration function provided we understand its rationale, its effect on human interactions and intimate connection with our goals and values. Blind dependency on technology can be self-defeating. Technology therefore should be considered as a means rather than an end in itself.

Liaison Individuals

Liaison individuals, sometimes referred to as "integrators", are individuals that may officially belong to any of the functional units of the organization but are given the responsibility for integrating the activities of two or more units.

Cross-functional Teams

Teams drawn form several functional areas. The effectiveness of integration depends on two major factors — knowledge and decision authority. Does the team have the authority to make decisions? Does it have the necessary knowledge? Have members of the team been able to confront their differences openly and establish sufficient consensus to provide effective collaboration?

Interpersonal Communication

Interpersonal communication is the common denominator in any integration mechanism. Promoting a greater flow of communications between all levels of management for greater interdisciplinary linkage and interlocking of functions. The organization is not only a production system, it is also a communication system. We have to include the directionality of communication, upward, downward and lateral. Communication includes formal and informal communication. We need to consider pathological forms of communication such as information deprivation, information overload, rumors and gossip.

2. Differentiation

Open systems develop in the direction of differentiation. Components of the system assume specialized functions that replace the global and diffuse patterns. Differentiation increases as we move up in the evolutionary hierarchy. At the lower levels of evolution, an organism senses the environment in a diffuse or global manner. At the top of the hierarchy is the human organism which has attained the highest level of biological and psychological differentiation. The human body possesses highly differentiated sensory modalities. Angler (1991) explains sensory differentiation: Humans and other mammals detect smells by using at least a thousand different genes that are active exclusively in nose cells ... the nose and brain together discriminate between the astringency (harshness) of lemon juice, the sweetness of a hyacinth and the sharp acidity of a skunk's spray. So many different receptors seem necessary to allow animals to smell. By comparison, the eye uses only three different types of receptors to recognize thousands or tens of thousands of colors. In the eye, there are photo-receptors that respond to red, green and blue. When viewing an object, the three different types of photoreceptor pass along signals of varying intensity, and the brain then combines and interprets the signals to tell pink from violet and from turquoise.

Thus, humans have been able to distinguish sounds, tastes, temperature, texture, pain and pleasure, pressure, speed, duration, etc. Further differentiation occurs within each modality. For example, the eye goes beyond differentiating objects from each other, to distinguishing colors, shades of colors, differences in speed of moving objects and the like. With such high degree of differentiation, humans have the potential to derive highly precise and varied information about the environment. That is how humans can be more selective and more efficient in dealing with the environment. Differentiation also occurs at a mental level. Memory, imagination and reasoning make it possible for us to extend our boundaries beyond the reaches of the senses. Thus we can distinguish past, present and future. The three distinct functions working together in a concerted fashion enable us to grasp actualities and consider possibilities. Thus we can respond efficiently to current happenings, and plan for the future. Learning extends our mental powers further.

We are concerned here with differentiation at the group level. The group interfaces with an environment that makes multiple demands on it. It is faced with problems of varying kinds. The organization cannot survive by global understanding of reality. Problems are getting increasingly more complex. We will have to specialize. That is to say, we have to move from general assessment of reality to sophisticated understanding. Organizations rely more and more on specialists to help provide more sophisticated solutions to its problems. Failure to differentiate may be taken as a symptom of deterioration whether in individuals or in social systems. So the issue of differentiation boils down to specialization. Specialization means developing expertise, Diversity becomes a necessity. The kind of diversity we recommend should include opinion diversity, diversity of perspective, of complementary views, not only diversity in professional specialization. This is because each group of specialists may end up by thinking alike and this is likely to be self-defeating. Often diversity takes place along ethnic or group membership. Such diversity leads to fragmentation and harms the solidarity of the system.

3. Interdependence

It is not possible to have both a high degree of differentiation and extremely precise integration within an organizational system. If integration is to proceed successfully, it must take place in conjunction with differentiation, since the two are actually inverse processes. Therefore, changes in subsystem components should be made in light of the integration between subsystem components and that the processes of differentiation and integration should constitute "an oscillating system in which each element continuously takes the other into account".

Assessment of Integrative Effort

Allen (1971) defined integrative effort as the amount of working time that managers devote to achieving integration. Through a comparison of high and low performing firms faced with high levels of environmental diversity, Allen found that the high level performing firms had high levels of integration and relatively low levels of integrative effort, while the low-performers were characterized by lower levels of differentiation that their environmental diversity suggested was required. Yet, the latter were found to devote more effort to integration while achieving a lower level of integration.

This seems to indicate that there are upper and lower limits to the benefits obtainable from investing time in integrative efforts. It would appear that those organizations which seemed to be performing poorly had passed this upper limit and were overloading communication channels rather than directing energies needed to deal with their own particular environments. Allen's research implies that management may spend too much time trying to develop collaboration among various specialized subsystems. Hence a balance must be found between interdependence among internal subunits while maintaining the degree of internal diversity necessary for dealing with a highly diverse environment. It follows that an open system should remain loosely joined in order to allow change to meet a diverse and changing environment.

RECURRENT SITUATIONS

Every great operation of war is unique. What is wanted is a profound appreciation of the actual event.

— Winston Churchill

1. Introduction

So far we have dealt with organizational processes in a general way. But organizational life includes more than general parameters of structure, leadership and the like. Organizations are complex environments that do not cease to generate all sorts of situations to which people must react. Some of these situations are recurrent while others are random and unexpected. I think it is important at the outset to define what we mean by 'situation'. A situation is a complex state of affairs that envelops individuals or groups. A situation is different from a stimulus. In fact a stimulus never exists in isolation from a situation even in the most contrived laboratory experiments. A leader does not respond to a stimulus, but to a global situation that consists of multiple interacting forces. The way a leader structures the totality of a situation in his mind will determine his subsequent intervention in that situation. But the outcome of the leader's action depends on the dynamics of the situation which of course includes the leader's inputs into it.

2. Entry Situations: A Typology

In this section I will describe a set of recurrent situations that leaders encounter in the course of their career. We call these situations "entry situations." That is when a manager is called upon to take charge of a group or an entire organization. In the eyes of the constituency the "new boss" will remain an outsider until he or she is accepted as a legitimate leader. The challenge of *becoming* the leader depends on the leader's sensitivity to the nature of the situation and the traditions of the constituency. Organizations can facilitate this process through mechanisms built into their traditions. The police and the army have established such traditions. Ceremonies consisting of predetermined rituals are performed. This is not always the case in other formal organizations. In the absence of such rituals, the new boss has to depend on his or her past experience and ingenuity in assessing the nature of the situational parameters. The power of situational forces could not be ignored.

It must be known that one becomes a member in a social system through an individual or a group in that system. Ideally, the first contact should be made through the individual in charge at the time or any authority figure representing the organization. There are horror stories of failure in this. I would like to relate an incident that I witnessed in the course of a consulting assignment in Korea. An English man heading a branch of an American bank happened to depend on a local official, the head of a department, in running the daily affairs of the branch. The local happened to be a fierce manager much feared and mistrusted by the employees. In effect, he isolated the new CEO from the entire body of employees. The new CEO put his trust in that manager without ever introducing himself to the rank-and-file. Rumor went around that the CEO was a "coward", totally controlled by the local officer. I happened to know that man. He was far from being a coward. In fact, he was one of the most adventurous men I have ever met in my life. At one time he headed a bank in an African country. Being a committed naturalist he would go on forays in the jungle exploring different types of plants and would face tigers. He would lie on his belly carrying his three year-old-daughter on his back. He once advised me on how to face a tiger myself, "just lay still and look straight at the eyes of the tiger. You would be safe." He graduated from Oxford University and has been an authority on insects and birds. Abiding by the typical British reserve, he "would avoid invading people's private sphere". So he would go hurriedly through a hall full of employees leading to his office. He would not greet anybody or talk to anybody "to avoid embarrassing them or interfere with their activities". Thus, the local manager could easily isolate the boss from the entire constituency. But the reason why the new boss accepted that state of affairs was that he had defined his role in the organization as a banker, not as leader — contacting high worth clients and public officials.

A typology of entry situations is worth mentioning at this point. So far I could identify five types that I encountered in my consulting and research experience. The reader would undoubtedly discover other types. I will provide below a brief description of each of the five types.

Successful Organization

This is the type of organization that could roughly be described as successful. Success is defined in terms of past achievements. As a result morale is high and work motivation is sustained. The rank-and-file attribute the success of the organization to the outgoing boss. He was kept in high regard by most people in the organization. It is reasonable to surmise that his departure would be experienced by the constituency as a loss and that any successor would be tolerated at best.

What would be the most important item in the agenda of the new boss? Common sense would provide the answer to this question — it is to reassure the constituency that he or she is more committed to continuity than to change. In other words, the new manager has to give clear signals that he is going to preserve, and buttress his predecessor's past achievements. Rushing to change would be inadvisable. Showing any sign of competitiveness with the departing CEO would be self defeating. This does not necessarily mean that no innovation would be possible. Rather, the issue would be a matter of proper timing. Any attempt to initiate a justifiable change has to wait until the new boss has been securely accommodated as a member. Membership is the first priority at this stage.

A case in point, a new CEO was to take over from a CEO that had led the organization through necessary dramatic changes. After five years of agonies, he managed to turn the organization around. When a new boss arrived, people were just beginning to enjoy the fruits of their success. The organization mission had been changed. So was the structure. The incoming CEO was fully aware of these facts, but he was *driven* to establish his presence. He formed 15 committees as task forces. His rationale was *to stir up* the organization. He arrives burdened by his own ideology and goodwill for *his* new constituency. The entire organization was turned into a laboratory of studies. People managed however to put up with his demands. They saw goodwill in his decisions and they were decent enough "to give him a chance". Meanwhile, he did not interfere with the existing power structure. Managers reporting to him saw his actions as "harmless nuisance" that interfered minimally with the overall functioning of the system. The situation would have been disastrous had the new boss tried to change course. Fortunately, he did not.

Failing Organization

This situation demands an opposite approach to the previous type. In fact the new boss is in a favorable position for authoritative action. He would have to depend more on his inner resources than on yielding to external demands. Uncertainty in this case comes from chaos and fluidity of the situation. Any intervention that counteracts the forces of entropy would be most appreciated. Speed in decision making is called for. Effective action of any kind, even if symbolic, would have a positive effect on the rank and file. However, quick intervention does not mean impulsive behavior. Action should be taken after quick assessment of the situation. A situation of this type should be dealt with as an emergency where any action is better than inaction. Errors ought to be tolerated but corrected quickly. Trial and error in such situations is more appropriate than pondered decisions.

Competitively Driven Organization

Often we find a reasonably successful organization where groups within may be fiercely competing with each other but somehow manage to master the art of *containment*. The organization may be perceived from outside as dynamic and vibrant in view of success despite occasional internecine conflicts. Managers are typically over-active and striving Top leadership has no other choice but yield to the power of a bunch of *prima donnas* who bring profit. The organization is profitable but vulnerable. Some prima donnas actually maintain power by blackmail. A new CEO coming into this climate has to be politically astute. He or she should not confront head on but every step has to be the result of calculation. It is common in such situations that competing managers would try to co-opt the new boss. He could be receptive without yielding to such attempts. He needs as much information as he can get from the approaches of different competing factions. But he is well advised to reach out to the silent majority. Sizing up the situation and gathering neutral coalition around him can provide objective inputs on the basis of which he may consider structural changes. Before making any structural changes, however, he must reach clear assessment of the status of the organization in the market, its strengths and its vulnerability.

Initiating a New Venture

A new venture requires a completely different mode of entry from the previous types. Building a new organization requires that the trusted individual behaves as an independent entrepreneur. Autonomy would be his greatest asset. But since he has been trusted by the authority that assigned the venture to him, he has to negotiate for the following: (a) a clear mandate; (b) sufficient resources, financial, material and otherwise; (c) sufficient autonomy and (c) time frame. The latter is particularly important. Quite often, time is ignored. A lot of problems are likely to arise for the manager who accepted the mandate and all needed resources but failed to negotiate for sufficient time for the delivery of agreed upon output. As "a good soldier", a manager may welcome a risky assignment but fails to secure agreement as to the time needed to fulfill the promise. The leader should not worry initially about structure. He has to select associates that already identify with him. Trust is of the essence. A small well-knit group is better than a large group. The power of face-to-face-group is of the essence. Experts can be drawn into the group one after the other as the need arises.

Dissolving an Organization

Dissolving an organization is one of the most challenging situations a leader may encounter in his entire career. The challenge is particularly threatening if the organization to be dissolved has been led by the person who is charged with dissolving it. The complexity of the leadership role comes to the foreground. Meanwhile the vulnerability of the leader is exposed. Multiple decisions have to be made: One is to announce the bad news to the rank and file. More often than not the decision has to be kept confidential for some time and the person in charge has to bear the burden of secrecy, withholding the information from loyal and dedicated subordinates; second, outplacement decisions; third, lay-off decisions and getting ready to deal with their legal aftermath.

3. Implications of the Typology

The situations described above demonstrate the poverty of the intrapersonal approach to leadership. Too much emphasis on the leader as a *cause* of events ignores the fact that the success of a leader in one context does not necessarily guarantee that he will achieve the same level of success or any success at all in different organizations or under different conditions. Each situation has its unique forces and imposes its imperatives. However, past experiences tend to have beneficial effects due to the natural phenomenon known in psychology as "transfer of training". This occurs when learning to do one task makes it easier to learn a second one. Transfer of training from one situation to another is enhanced if conditions of both situations are similar enough to allow extrapolation. Experience is defined in many studies as the time spent in a job or in an organization. This definition does not capture all the important elements of what one might mean by experience. Other aspects might include the richness of the experience, its relevance, diversity, or what actually has been learned from previous situations.

We must also bear in mind that past experience may block new learning. That is when the leader makes the mistake of repeating past successful actions in new situations that are very different from earlier situations. Examples from history abound. General Dwight Eisenhower has been judged by academics as a very poor leader when he was appointed President of Columbia University. In fact President Harry Truman judged him to be a "shameful failure as President of the United States". Truman also felt that "generals tend to make very poor presidents".[17]

In the final analysis, the intrapersonal resources of a leader do not exist in isolation from the social context. The leader's perception of situational parameters was found to be more predictive of person-situation match effects than were objective assessments of those variables. In other words how structured the leader perceived a task to be or how supportive subordinates were seen to be proved to be a better predictor than were the objective nature of the task or the actual reports of those subordinates.

---

[17] Miller, M. (1974). *Plain Speaking: An Oral Biography of Harry S. Truman*. New York: Berkley Books.

Interface Groups

1. Definition of Small Groups

By interface group we mean a small group in which members come into direct contact with each other over a period of time. Members have equal opportunities to see and interact with each other. There is agreement that seven is the maximum size that a group can attain and still retain the characteristics of a small group. More than seven the group tends to split into sub groups. It is through small groups that members of the organization relate to the entire organization. Small groups mediate the relationship between individuals and the global system. Meanwhile groups are structured in larger units, whether as departments, divisions, or branches. Some groups are integral parts of the enduring structure of the organization. Others are of a shorter life cycle, such as project teams, task forces, or committees. In fact members of the organization may commute among different groups while being considered as permanent members of certain groups. A sort of tumultuous traffic characterizes any organization.

It is commonly accepted that "a group is more than the sum total of its individual members". When people form a group, many forces, other than what individuals carry within them, are set in motion: identification with a common purpose, exchange of information; influence attempts; conflict situations; power struggle; group pressure; development of norms; exchanges with other groups, patterns of coping with external demands and pressures. These forces make up the life course of any group. In addition each group will in due time develop a distinctive character. That character could not be predicted from what we may already know about the individual characters of the group members.

The task of leading interface groups is very different from leading single individuals or the large organization of which the groups are components. Therefore, to be able to lead a group, the leader must make a conscious effort to shift attention away from individuals and focus instead on the group as a collective entity. But this of course requires prior knowledge of the basic parameters which define a group. The leader must have prior knowledge of certain phenomena that are common to all groups. The leader will have to watch out for these phenomena as the group process unfolds. Managers often talk — and may even know a lot — about "group" dynamics. But very few seem able to use this knowledge in monitoring group behavior, let alone exerting influence on it. Often, the group leader continues to monitor, and respond to, behavior of individuals losing sight of what goes on within the group as a whole or between the group and other groups. As a result, many managers who admittedly work hard often fail to utilize the group as a vital resource in the service of both individuals and organizations. I conclude that managers' need for training in this field is both compelling and urgent.

Formal leaders of small groups are not the only source of influence. Research shows that leadership traits are not necessarily confined to the acknowledged leader, but may be widely distributed throughout the group. This is evidenced by the specific initiative that group members exhibit — providing pertinent information, asking questions, clarifying facts, offering suggestions, or mediating in conflict situations. Research further suggests that members of effective teams appear to have relatively more leadership potential than members of less effective teams (Hall, 1983; Garland & Barry, 1990). A well-developed group forces its traditions on a new leader. Some leaders are absorbed by the established group; others are assimilated and follow group traditions.

Studies by the US army showed that leadership varies from one situation to another. It was not always the most assertive individual who dominated the group process, although many of those who rose to leadership position were assertive. The leadership position sometimes shifted from one individual to another. For example, a man who took the lead in discussing the problem might lose his place when attention was turned to actually carrying out the tasks required for its solution (Sherif & Sherif, 1953).

2. Transitory Teams

One of the most striking features of change in the current business environment is the increased reliance on temporary teams. Such teams are formed for the purpose of attaining definite objectives after which the teams disband. Temporary work teams include task forces, brain storming teams, crisis intervention groups, and negotiation teams. Then there are hundreds of meetings, regular and irregular. The typical American manager spends 30% to 70% of the day in meetings. In many meetings 20% of the people do 80% of the talking.[18] Members of such teams represent different disciplines in the same firm or in different firms. Quite often participants in these teams are strangers to each other and have no legitimate authority over one another. They have therefore, to rely exclusively on their personal resources in their attempts to exert influence on one another. Increased reliance on temporary teams is due to the fact that management began to realize a number of things:

First, current formal structures cannot adequately cope with the increasing complexity of business problems. Resolving such problems call for maximum exchange among specialists of disparate disciplines. Second, due to the unpredictability of the market, task forces have to be quickly assembled to deal with the unexpected events. It is evident that work in such transitory and discontinuous settings presents serious challenge to managers who are used to settle in the same position for a relatively long time, supervising the same work force, and dealing most of the time with regular and "expected" problems. In a stable environment precedence and past experience combined with goodwill could help. The situation is quite different now. That is why there seems to be a compelling need for training programs to enable managers to meet this new challenge. General training in leadership is too general to help. Training in running small groups promises better results.

---

[18] *Fortune* magazine, March 23, 1992.

Third, senior leaders do not have direct influence on temporary teams. Conversely, the teams have influence on the overall performance of their respective organizations. On the other hand, the success of the teams depends on the flow of influence among its members. Leaders at the group level are effective to the extent that they facilitate participation. Success in running such teams requires skills different than those required of leaders of large groups.

3. Informal Groups

A small group can be either formal or informal. Informal groups cannot be located on the organization's chart. They circulate insidiously and spontaneously outside the formal organization structure. Informal groupings tend to be fluid and the interactions within them are more personal and intimate. They are formed by virtue of proximity within the organizational space but are independent of the organization structure. I must also include in this category all sorts of cliques, coalitions and elite groups that play a strong influence on corporations and political organizations. Many writers argue that leadership figures count so much less than the élites they represent and that it doesn't much matter which is in office. National or corporate leaders tend to form some sort of fraternity with their counterparts in other countries or corporations.

4. Dyadic Structures

The belief that a leader is a totally independent individual or lone ranger is a myth. No leader can rise or sustain his authority by being totally independent. Often, we find a leader moving up in the organization or the nation as a nucleus of a clique. Even then we note the emergence of a dyadic structure. A leader moves with one other figure forming a structure that acquires exclusive boundaries. This is what is known as the dyadic structure or the "alter ego" phenomenon. Here are some examples: General Robert Lee and Stonewall Jackson, a historical example in the US. In Asia there is the example of Chairman Mao and his illustrious Zhou Enlai. In Indonesia we find Sukarno-Hatta alliance. In the field of psychology we may cite the example of Freud and Jung even though the dyad broke up when the relationship soured. From the Middle East there is Nasser and his confidante Hussein Heikel. The alter ego does not have to be an associate in the same business but an outsider, sometimes even a lover or mistress: Hitler and Eva Brown; Mussolini and his mistress. Both couples lived and died together. A striking example in history is the relationship between President Lyndon Johnson and his driver.

A dyad is a complementary relationship in which two individuals engage in different behaviors, with the behavior of one serving as the stimulus for the behavior of the other. In the complementary relationship both parties assume different roles, one being dominant and the other submissive, one the superior and the other the subordinate. Dyadic structures stem from the fact that no human is complete. An individual has to be complemented or confirmed by at least one other person. Together, they form a unit that transcends the individuality of either. Sometimes the dyad is rightly called "composite character". Each dyad acquires its own identity and peculiarities.

Sometimes dyadic relationships are an integral part of the culture: such as teacher and student, doctor and patient, apprentice and master. Some dyadic relationships assume symbiotic quality where each member of the dyad is dependent on the other for certain essential features. Some are less strong and called conjugal rather than symbiotic. Max Schiller identified several forms of dyadic bonds. Some dyads are pathological while others are synergistic. We must also note a related phenomenon which is that of "dyadic rivals". In a fiercely competitive world of business or politics, every leader needs a protagonist as much as he or she needs an alter ego. Examples from modern history: In the political field in the US we may cite the example of Lyndon Johnson and Robert Kennedy. A famous example in business is Pepsi's Roger Enrico and Coke's Roberto Goizueta. They were seen by observers to be symbols of their world's most ruthless business war.

5. Leadership among Groups

In large institutions, a group may stand out as "leading subsystem" defined by Thelen (1960)[19] as a component system whose output exerts

---

[19] D. Katz & R. L. Kahn, *The Social Psychology of Organizations*, Second Edition, Jossey-Bass, 1978.

the greatest influence on the inputs of other component systems and through this, controls the interactions of the entire organization, the "supra-system". Thelen observes that sub-systems may vary in this characteristic during periods of rapid organizational growth, though a coordinating system having inputs and outputs may be permanently leading. During growth, the leading system may be the latest system to develop in the sense that it tends to be the "executive seat" for it obtains feedback and stimulation from all the other systems; it is the system best able to mediate between internal and external demands, and thus "to guide the locomotion of the organism as a whole". The special asset of the leading group may be expertise or capital or any other source of power.

6. Subordinates' Influence

According to Hollander (1993) leader and follower constitute interdependent reciprocal systems. In a fundamental way the leader's legitimacy and ultimate influence depends on his or her standing with followers. Followers provide opportunities and pose constraints, thus determining the scope of action available to the leader. The constraints include: lack of skill, lack of work motivation, resistance to change, and withholding necessary feedback. These constraints are not necessarily imposed consciously or intentionally. Sometimes this may be the case. Woodrow Wilson has this to say about the influence of subordinates:

> The actions of subordinates have important implications for the fulfillment of the needs and goals of the leader. Leaders with poorly performing subordinates are regarded as poor leaders. This enhances the leader's need to ascribe responsibility for poor performance to subordinate disposition, especially when results associated with that performance are extreme ... When an entire team performs poorly, negative evaluations of the leader may be enhanced.[20]

---

[20] Quoted by Tulis, 1987.

7. Effect of the Office on the Leader

An office constitutes a complex set of circumstances surrounding the office holder: the authority invested in the position, the daily tasks he undertakes, the people he has to encounter in the course of his work, the prestige of the office and how the leader reacts to it, and the daily routine determined by the position. Each office has its unique dynamics. It generates both challenges and opportunities. Success or failure of the office holder in handling them will determine subsequent decisions and reaction of followers and the public.

Psychologists refer to the "dynamogenic" force of a stimulus that unlocks the energies of a person. We can use the term in describing the influence of an office on the leader, with the proviso that the office is not just a stimulus. Rather, it is a complex situation that generates a barrage of stimuli every moment of the working day, and the office holder must deal with them. And the leader deals with them by marshalling all the resources available to him including his past experience. Meanwhile, a lot of learning takes place in the course of a leader's tenure. William James points out that[21]

> A new position of responsibility will usually show a man to be a far stronger creature than was supposed. Cromwell's and Grants careers are stock examples of how war will wake a man up. (p. 48)

What are the factors that account for the "dynamogenic" power of an office? A number of factors come to mind:

First factor is access to information: The office provides a view of reality that may be more global than the view available to individuals in the lower rungs of the hierarchy. Availability of such information at any time may give the office holder alternative opportunities for action. On the negative side, it may give the office holder the illusion of omniscience. The position may also conceal a great deal of information that may be vital for decision making. Often the next layer of leaders may actively isolate top leaders from the rank-and-file and act as filters of information, thus reducing the ultimate power of the office or sabotage the leader's efforts.

---

[21] James, W. (1947). *Selected Papers on Philosophy*. London: J. M. Dent & Sons. First published 1917.

Second factor is length of tenure: time spent in a position of authority should also be considered. A long tenure may provide opportunities for the leader to gather more information and to strengthen his hold on power. On the other hand, a leader may develop rigidities that reduce his responsiveness to change. Length of tenure may also reveal to the constituency more unfavorable information about the leader.

Third factor is the method that brought the leader to the position. The leader may gain access to the office through election or appointment. Election and appointment create different psychological climates affecting both leaders and followers. Once in office, elected leaders are likely to feel obligated to meet the expectations of the voters or promises the leader may have made. The voters who brought the leaders to the office expect to be paid back. As a result, leaders may not feel totally free to exercise authority as they should. It takes a very confident and strong-willed leader to rely on his judgment rather than surrender to group's expectations.

Fourth factor is the degree of perceived success or failure of the leader. I noted earlier that the office may isolate the leader from the constituency or from lower layers of leadership. This is particularly evident in the case of leaders who have achieved success. Success boosts the leader's confidence. Impressed by the leader's success, temporary as it might be, followers may exaggerate the capabilities of the leader to the point that the latter ceases to exercise self-criticism. The leader may ultimately ignore, or deny real shortcomings in himself or in his policies. We must, however, note that some leaders are more vulnerable to this danger than others. Ego-centricity and narcissism are the most serious impediments that afflict a leader.

The Organization as Environment

… When studied narrowly in himself by anthropologists or jurists, man is a tiny, even a shrinking, creature. His over pronounced individuality conceals from our eyes the whole to which he belongs; as we look at him our minds incline to break nature up into pieces and to forget both its deep inter-relations and its measureless horizons: we incline to all that is bad in anthropocentrism. And it is this that still leads scientists to refuse to consider man as an object of scientific scrutiny except through his body.

The time has come to realize that an interpretation of the universe — even a positivist one — remains unsatisfying unless it covers the interior as well as the exterior of things; mind as well as matter. The true physics is that which will, one day, achieve the inclusion of man in his wholeness in a coherent picture.

— Teilhard de Chardin (1975)[22]

Organizational Dimensions

The organization is set up to serve a more-or-less defined mission. In time, however, it will inevitably end by becoming an environment in its own right thus transcending its central mission. The organization like any social environment is multi-dimensional. The following dimensions

---

[22] de Chardin, Teilhard (1975). *The Phenomenon of Man* (transl. B. Wall). New York: Harper & Row. [Original publication in French, 1959.]

characterize any organization irrespective of its primary purpose or mission.

Economic Dimension

The economic dimension covers the financial aspects of the organization, its capital position, its overall cost base. The latter includes the cost and value of specific activities, the way those activities are executed; the divergence between expense and revenue growth. To what extent does cost reduction go with enhancing productivity? Does it go with increasing revenues without increasing cost base?

Legal Dimension

The organization is bound by laws both local and global. Organization's survival does not depend exclusively on its internal structure, internal laws and procedures. The organization depends on many other organizations — suppliers, clients, competitors and many others, not to mention civil organizations and various publics.

Political Dimension

The term 'political' is used here in the classical sense, a derivative of *polis* or city state. Organizations are systems of interdependent roles. Each position is differentiated by fairly precise assignments of authority and prestige. Furthermore, organizations are composed of many sub-hierarchies, each bound together by authority, interests, and values in a way similar to the total organization (Presthus, 1978).[23]

Power relations govern interactions in organizations. Harmony is no more than an ideal that organizations strive to reach but they rarely do in reality. This is because organizations are highly diversified systems fraught with contradictions and conflicting demands made upon them from diverse quarters internal and external. Conflict is inevitable. It arises over legitimate issues, whether strategic or tactical. If unresolved, conflicts often degenerate into personality conflict. Furthermore,

---

[23] Presthus, R. (1978). *The Organizational Society,* revised edition. New York: St. Martin's Press.

organizations are microcosms of society in terms of class stratification, interest groups and diverse value orientations. There will always be conflict over scarce resources, competing and power struggle.

Information Dimension

Decision making at any level of the organization hierarchy depends on the availability of information and the speed with which the information could be retrieved. Many decisions must be made under conditions of uncertainty. Weick[24] points out that the process of organizing is a process of reduction of uncertainty:

> The basic raw materials on which organizations operate are informational inputs that are ambiguous, uncertain, [and] equivocal. Whether the information is embedded in tangible raw materials, recalcitrant customers, assigned tasks, or union demands, there are many possibilities or sets of outcomes that *might* occur. Organizing serves to narrow the range of possibilities, to reduce the number of "might occurs". The activities of organizing are directed towards the establishment of a workable level of certainty. An organization attempts to transform equivocal information into a degree of unequivocality with which it can work and to which it is accustomed. This means that absolute certainty is seldom required. It also means that there can be enormous differences among organizations and industries with respect to the level of clarity that they regard as sufficient for action. (p. 6)

Learning Dimension

Survival of any organization depends on its ability to learn. The learning process is very complex. Learning includes soliciting suggestions and opinions from clients and staff, and from continued dialogue with experts and learning institutions. Learning also depends on the ability of the organization to detect obsolescence and devise mechanisms to correct for it. Professional training may be such a mechanism. Training can pay off only if the graduates of training

---

[24]Weick, K. E. (1979). *The Social Psychology of Organizing*, second edition. New York: Random House.

programs are enabled to utilize the fresh skills they gain from training programs. Then there is the organization's ability to attract, and retain talented professionals. Training programs have to be complemented by strategies of hiring new blood.

Creating an environment that fosters innovation is not less vital than formal training programs. Most training programs focus narrowly on the skills directly related to job performance. Innovation in performance requires expansion of training beyond such skills. General knowledge provides depth for immediate skills. Expanding horizons of professional people is an important determinant of innovation. Lee Kun Hee, Chairman of the Korean Group Samsung seems to have captured this notion. One of his pet projects for broadening the international experience of Samsung managers is to dispatch 400 bright junior employees annually to different countries of their choice at full pay and expense to do nothing but travel and soak up the local cultures. The notion of paying young people not to work both bothered old hands at Samsung, but Lee sees it as a prudent investment for the future.[25]

There is no learning without unlearning. The latter is achieved in a culture that adopts a self-critical attitude. A tradition of self-criticism enables the organization to detect errors early enough to be corrected. Popper (1999)[26] has this to say about the role of trial and error in learning:

> ... the adoption of a critical attitude, and the realization that not only trial but also error is necessary. And [we] *must learn not only to expect mistakes, but consciously to search for them.* We all have an unscientific weakness for being always in the right and this weakness seems to be particularly common among professional and amateur politicians. But the only way to apply something like scientific method in politics is to proceed on the assumption that there can be no political move which has no drawbacks, no undesirable consequences. To look out for these mistakes, to find them, to bring them into the open, to analyse them, and to learn from them, this is what a scientific politician as well as a political scientist must do. Scientific method in politics means that the great art of convincing ourselves that we

[25] Kraar, R. (1994, June 1). The Way of Chairman Lee. *Asiaweek*, pp. 32–39.
[26] Popper, K. R. (1999). *The Poverty of Historicism*. London: Routledge (first published 1957).

have not made any mistakes, of ignoring them, of hiding them, and of blaming others for them, is replaced by the greater art of accepting the responsibility for them, of trying to learn from them, and of applying this knowledge so that we may avoid them in the future. (p. 88)

Enhancing institutional memory is another mechanism that enables the organization to be truly a "learning system". Knowledge survives only in the minds of individuals. Only sharing knowledge and passing it to next generations constitutes what we call organization memory. So much individual experiences are lost to the organization if the organization lacks a mechanism of preserving them and retrieving them as the need arises. A deplorable phenomenon I witnessed in companies that have operations in foreign countries — the employees who have spent a good number of years overseas are never consulted upon reassignment at home. Their experience gets buried as if it has never been acquired.

Socio-cultural Dimension

Many formal and informal inputs merge to develop what is referred to as organizational culture. Technology, type of products or services, and job structure provide inputs into the culture of the organization. For example, a company which provides product with a short life cycle and relies on computer technology will have a different culture than a company which provides a long life cycle product and relies on interpersonal and face-to-face technology. Leadership style and superior–subordinate relationships affect the overall climate of the organization. Identification of workers with the organization and morale are factors to be included in our understanding of the societal dimension. The legal power of the organization may be strengthened or weakened by the informal structure of the organization as a community of people. Often informal structure complements, or corrects for the rigidity of the formal structure. Through informal structure, organizations may be able to respond to situations for which their formal structures are inadequate. Another societal factor is the organization's commitment to the public — the extent to which the organization is committed to the well-being of the society and the environment at large.

Interdependence of the Dimensions

The dimensions are not mutually exclusive. They are different ways of looking at an organization. No organization could be called exclusively economic or exclusively social or legal. The organization is a complex environment with different manifestations. The main thrust of the organization is determined directly by its mission but all other aspects outlined above will operate as background for the primary thrust and may even act as modifying attributes. Buzan *et al.*[27] use the analogy of lenses through which we may look at the organization from different perspectives:

> … [dimensions] are views of the whole system through some selective lens that highlights one particular aspect of the relationship and interaction among all of its constituent units. The metaphor of a lens is quite accurate. In the physical world, one can look at an object using many different types of "lenses," ranging from the naked eye and telescopes, through infra-red sensors and radars, to X-ray machines and electron microscopes. In each case the lens is either sensitive to different types, or wavelengths, of energy (e.g., infra-red and X-ray), or else sensitive to the same type of energy in a different way (e.g., microscope and telescope). Thus even though the object observed remains the same (ignoring Heisenberg), different lenses highlight different aspects of its reality. The naked eye sees mostly exterior shape and color. The infra-red sees the pattern of heat. The X-ray sees the pattern of physical density. The electron microscope sees molecular structure. The function of sectors is the same as that of lenses: each one gives us a view of the whole that emphasizes some qualities, and de-emphasizes, or even hides completely, others.

The organization as a whole entity interfaces with other systems in a common environment. Wholeness is not something that happens naturally. Rather, it is the end product of organizing processes and efforts of integration. Integration mechanisms must be devised to cause wholeness to happen. Multidimensionality of the organization argues against centralization of leadership in a single individual or group of

---

[27]Buzan, B., Jones, C. and Little, R. (1993) *The Logic of Anarchy: Neorealism to Structural Realism.* New York: Columbia University Press.

powerful individuals. Furthermore, leadership should entail more than striving to achieve the narrow purpose of the organization. In fact the realization of the core mission of the organization is impossible without sustaining the organization in its totality. In other words leadership as a social process has to match the complexity of the organization.

Modes of Existence in Organizations

First and foremost, the individual, like Leibniz's monads, should mirror the world. Why? I cannot say why, except that knowledge and comprehensiveness appear to me glorious attributes, in virtue of which I prefer Newton to an oyster. The man who holds concentrated and sparkling within his own mind, as within a *camera obscura*, the depths of space, the evolution of the sun and planets, the geological ages of the earth, and the brief history of humanity appears to me to be doing what is distinctively human and what adds most to the diversified spectacle of nature.

— Bertrand Russell[28]

1. Membership

Becoming a member is a process that newcomers to any organization go through from the time they *join in* to the time they make an exit either by choice or by dismissal. The organization is a complex and evolving system with identifiable structure and dynamic interactive components. Membership is the key to social life. This is true for all social systems irrespective of size, purpose or history.

Membership is a continuous process initiated by a contract. A contract belongs to the past, namely to the time when the person

---

[28]Bertrand Russell (1992). *Education and the Social Order.* London: Routledge (first published 1932).

joined in. At best it is a declaration of promise about the future. Such promise does not tell us much about membership as a *lived* experience.

Partial Inclusion

Individuals do not exist in the organization as articles exist *inside* a container. Rather, they exist *in relation to* other individual members and groups that make up the organization. Becoming a member in any group poses a challenge to the individual who would naturally abhor anonymity or the fate of being reduced to a number. Fortunately, the individual does not have to give up completely his identity, nor does he have to become totally anonymous even though in certain groups such as fanatic gangs, members' personal identities have to be submerged in the group or de-individuated. Furthermore, assuming membership in a given organization does not forfeit membership elsewhere. Multiple memberships expand the scope of an individual's life and avails him or her of varied resources for further growth, thus sharpening one's sense of personal identity. This is of course true provided (a) the individual is capable of limiting memberships to a manageable few, and (b) is able to establish optimum balance in meeting the demands of different memberships.

The human person cannot lead a complete life by holding a single membership in a single social group. Beyond a limited period of childhood dependency, the individual usually seeks memberships in varied spheres of social life. It follows that no organization has the power to claim the totality of the human person. I like to refer to this phenomenon as the principle of *partial inclusion*. What matters for individuals is a membership that enhances continued growth and sharpens personal identity. And what matters to the organization is quality membership, i.e., significant contribution to its mission. In fact neither the organization nor the individual member would benefit from total inclusion. I find direct support of this view in a statement that a Nobel Laureate, Kenneth Arrow made:

> An organization is typically composed of changing individuals. Now any individual typically has access to many communication channels, of which this particular organization is only one. In particular, education is such channel. Thus the organization is getting the benefit of a considerable amount of information

which is free to it. Even though the code of the organization may make the internal transmission of such information costly, if there is enough of it, the behavior of the organization will change. In particular, new items will appear on the organization's agenda.[29] (p. 59)

I must stress, however, that multiple memberships does not imply that the individual allocates parts of himself or herself to different groups. The individual participates as a whole person in various social systems. The organization cannot, and should not try to, *fully* assimilate its members. The extent and depth of inclusion required by organizations vary according to the mission of the organization and the nature of its norms. The military, for example, requires almost total inclusion during an initial specified period after which the individual is allowed to commute between the barracks and the outside world. Typically a Japanese firm demands more inclusion than an American firm. Membership in secret societies is exclusionary — the member may be required to relinquish all other affiliations, family affiliation included.

Affiliation Needs[30]

Membership has two aspects to it: legal or contractual, and psychological or subjective. The legal aspect is concrete enough to be grasped. It is simply the degree to which the member accepts and abides by the rules, regulations, and expectations spelt out in the contractual agreement. The subjective aspect is the individual's *identification* with the organization. As such, membership is the *experience* of affiliation or belonging. It takes place at any or all of three levels — cognitive, affective and volitional. Membership as experience starts as the newcomer is assigned a job in one, or more, of the work groups. For some members the legal bond provides sufficient basis for settling in and performing the assigned role. For others, however, membership must transcend the contractual commitment and have personal meaning.

---

[29]Arrow, K. J. (1974). *The Limits of Organization*. New York: W. W. Norton.
[30]Schachter, S. (1959). *The Psychology of Affiliation: Experimental Studies of the Sources of Gregariousness*. Stanford, CA: Stanford University Press.

Meaningful membership is vital for the person's sense of identity. "The individual," says Herbert Mead "is what he is, just in so far as he is a member of society, involved in the social process of experience and activity, and thereby socially controlled in his conduct." We get a sense of how important membership is to the individual if we ponder the bitterness implicit in the vocabulary of exclusion: banished, expelled, ostracized, shunned, snubbed, defrocked, deported, disowned, exiled or driven out. Nothing would compensate for the tragedy of losing membership in a group other than membership in another group.

Decline of Identification

In modern times, identification with the organization has greatly diminished or totally replaced by a contractual obligation based on the price system. In other words membership may be sustained on the basis of economic necessity. Several factors contribute to this state of affairs: One is the organization's increased reliance on technocratic expertise, which gives rise to rampant elitism. Airline pilots may consider themselves the core of aviation industry forgetting that flying a plane is made possible by efforts of various groups on the ground. Doctors may assign more weight to the medical role than the nursing role. In financial institutions, investment experts may regard themselves more relevant than say *back office* workers. The academic staff in a university may look down at the administrative staff. Elitism is endemic in most modern organizations. And in its extreme form, elitism gives rise to the phenomenon of *inverse identification* — elite groups expecting the organization to identify with them rather than the other way round.

The second factor is membership in labor unions, which competes with membership in the organization. Often several competing unions pervade the same organization. The third factor is the wave of mergers and acquisitions, which has devastating effect on the experience of long-term affiliation. The fourth factor is globalization that transfers power from states to multinational corporations.

We should bear in mind that individuals do not relate to the total organization directly. They become members through primary work groups. In due course they join a variety of informal groups from which they learn much about the organization. Members' experience in groups, whether formal or informal, mediates their ultimate attitudes towards the organization. These attitudes are not fixed.

Several forces help shape the newcomer's experience: first, the immediate supervisor's effort to integrate the newcomer into the organization as a contributing agent. Unfortunately supervisors tend to be more superior-oriented than subordinate-oriented. Typically, most of their time and effort is devoted to meeting the demands of their superiors. Supervisors may also be more organization-oriented than subordinate-oriented such as when they appear to be more solicitous of the organization at the expense of the welfare of their immediate subordinates. This state of affairs, I believe, is responsible for the prevalence of two deficiencies in many organizations — inadequate supervision and near absence of apprenticeship.

Second, peers play a significant role in shaping the newcomer's concept of, and attitude towards, the organization. Relationship among peers could be cooperative, competitive or adversarial. Management style of group leaders tips the balance in favor of one or the other of such outcomes. Often healthy relationship among peers compensates for the weakened relationship with the immediate boss. I have been told by several professionals in more than one organization that despite the remoteness of the immediate boss, they would not leave the organization thanks to their "inspiring coworkers".

Third, members' identification with their respective groups depends on the perceived status of these groups within the organization. Groups vary as to their attitudes towards the organization and towards each other. Groups are often in conflict with the organization or at least ambivalent in their attitudes towards the organization. Presthus (1978)[31] challenges the human relations view which defines the organization as "cooperative system" composed of many intimate work groups which meet individual needs for identification. He notes:

> While small groups undoubtedly meet such needs, it seems equally clear that their members do not necessarily identify with the larger organization. With rare exceptions, the influence of any given individual on this level is inconsequential, and he

---

[31] Presthus, R. (1978). *The Organizational Society*, revised edition. New York: St. Martin's Press.

knows it. As the Hawthorne studies found, the small group often plays a *protective* role, shielding its members from real or imaginary threats of management. Small group relations are often compensatory and negative; they may even underscore the employee's estrangement from the larger organization. A study of the automobile industry concludes: "When the worker discussed his relations with other workers and reported social interaction, such as joking, gossiping, or general conversation, he mentioned them chiefly as a fortunate *counterbalance and compensation* for the disliked features of his job." (p. 201)

Fourth, organization policies and managerial practices convey directly or indirectly something about the individual's worth. Fifth, public image of the organization influences the member's identification with the organization. Members derive pride or shame depending on how the organization is perceived by other organizations or by the public at large. Somehow members like to be affiliated to an organization that is perceived as a respectable institution.

Problematic Issues

The concept of membership on the surface seems straightforward and easy to comprehend. However, it does not take much thinking before we are confronted with perplexing issues. It is easy, for example, to think of employees as members of a given firm. But consider members of the organization board. Can we consider them members in the same way employees are, even though they hold paid positions in other organizations? How about regular clients without whose *loyalty* the organization would cease to exist? Or consider an educational institution such as the university. Who are the main members of the university? An easy answer is the employees, the administrators, the trustees, and the teaching staff. How about students for whom the university has been created? We become even more perplexed if we ask similar questions about patients in a hospital or nuns in a convent or convicts in prison or even children in a family. These questions suggest that the notion of membership raises compelling questions. The notion of social roles comes to our rescue. Let us then try to define what is meant by social roles.

2. Social Roles

A role is a social arrangement whereby membership is made *relevant* to the organization's mission. The organization survives through diverse individuals and groups that assume diverse roles meshing more or less cohesively with the mission of the organization. Thus individuals are not just members, but role holders. Naturally the newcomers acquire membership in the entire organization through job structure and participation in activities within primary work groups. How much the individual will actually feel that his or her membership extends beyond the primary groups will depend on the conditions in primary groups and how organizational policies pertaining to personnel are interpreted by the members.

In some organizations, such as the military, roles are tightly structured and standardized. Indoctrination in the military aims at the suppression of civilian habits and attitudes and replacing them by military habits. Indoctrination period is followed by intensive training. In less structured organizations, initiation of membership takes a less rigid form — brief orientation sessions including the signing of employment contracts. Thereafter the new employee is left to his own devices. Acquisition of a role marks the passage from anonymity to differentiated membership.

A role is a complex construct that consists of three components: first component is *responsibility* — what the member is expected to contribute to the overall enterprise. The assumption is that the person has been hired on the basis of skills and abilities that would enable him or her to contribute to the organization as quickly as possible. There is also the understanding that the new member may not be able to contribute fully upon joining. The organization must therefore provide orientation and training to facilitate and maximize the member's contribution in due course. In other words, responsibility defines the person's relevance to the organization. Job structure concretizes the component we call responsibility.

The second component is *authority*. Authority is a set of rules or principles that define the scope of powers invested in the member's position. Thus, a member is *authorized* to make demands on other people within or outside the system. Authority can also be defined as the power to demand cooperation, or even compliance, from certain other people. Authority ought to be seen as a resource that enables members to fulfill their responsibilities or undertake their duties. In this sense authority is a necessity, not a luxury. It is not the exclusive property of special types of people that we call leaders. Even a slave must have certain scope of freedom to be able to meet the master's expectations. Slavery does not turn the slave into a machine. The master depends on the slave's available energies and skills. Naturally, the slave's margin of freedom increases in time in proportion to the level of the slave's skill and consequently the master's dependency on his output.

The third component of a role is *accountability*. Accountability fulfills two functions. On one hand, it regulates or limits the use of authority. On the other hand, it defines the relative position of the individual in the chain of command. Accountability like responsibility and authority is never fixed. It develops in time in conjunction with the changes that take place in the leader-follower relationship. As Sherif has noted,

> The power invested in the leader is not arbitrary; it has to be used within certain bounds. If these bounds are violated, the leadership position is subject to various kinds of reactions from the rest of the organization. The leadership position itself is a position within the organization and not outside of it with complete freedom of direction. (pp. 43, 44)

It is important at this point to stress the *relational nature* of the notion of role. It is a mechanism of ordering daily transactions that must take place between interdependent parties. This is based on the fact that the quality of a person's work has consequences for another person or persons. Meanwhile the three role components should be interpreted as actual *activities* of exchange. For example, responsibility refers to actual activities a worker must undertake. Authority defines actual demands the role holder is expected to make on other fellow workers who also have parallel authority. Finally, accountability defines the restraints the role holder must exercise in dealing with other fellow workers. Imbalance in role components disrupts the relations among holders of interdependent set of roles. Considerable interpersonal conflict can be traced to variations in role imbalance.

Dual Role of Students

Let us now turn to the questions we raised earlier about membership in connection with students in the university and others such as prison inmates and patients in hospitals. Let us see how we can answer these questions in the light of role components. Starting with students, I pointed out that membership alone does not provide an answer to the question as to whether they could be considered consumers or clients. If we consider them consumers, it follows that education is a commodity. According to this conception, students' responsibility would be to pay tuition in return for education. Their responsibility would be to study for a specified number of years at the end of which they are awarded a diploma that may or may not qualify them to join the work force. This view ignores the principle of *partial inclusion*. It also ignores the fact that the students have a role to play as citizens of their respective countries. Are they supposed to put their citizenship on hold until graduation? History teaches us that students all over the world spearhead national struggle for independence or for civil rights. They fulfill their responsibility as citizens often in a manner that outweighs their responsibility as learners. External circumstances demand sometimes significant shifts between roles. Many world leaders, especially in Third World countries, started their political career as activists during their student years. And yet once they become statesmen, they become intolerant — to say the least — of students' participation in the political life of their country. Given that students are responsible citizens besides being learners the case may be made that they have a voice in running the affairs of the university. How much participation should the students undertake will depend on the particular circumstances of each university.

The function of the university as a social institution in a particular country should also be taken into consideration. Therefore, the issue is not whether a member should play a role — this is taken for granted — but how a role should be defined. And the role definition should be congruous with the organization mission. Furthermore the role definition should not violate the member's legitimate roles outside the organization.

Individuals as Citizens

Bertrand Russell (1932)[32] stresses the difference between being an individual in the abstract and a citizen:

> The elements of knowledge and emotion in the perfect individual as we have been portraying him are not essentially social. It is only through the will and through the exercise of power that the individual whom we have been imagining becomes an effective member of the community. And even so the only place which the will, as such, can give to a man is that of dictator. The will of the individual considered in isolation is the god-like will which says 'let such things be'. The attitude of the citizen is a very different one. He is aware that his will is not the only one in the world, and he is concerned, in one way or another, to bring harmony out of the conflicting wills that exist within his community. The individual as such is self-subsistent, while the citizen is essentially circumscribed by his neighbours. With the exception of Robinson Crusoe we are of course all in fact citizens, and education must take account of this fact. But it may be held that we shall ultimately be better citizens if we are first aware of all our potentialities as individuals before we descend to the compromises and practical acquiescences of the political life. The fundamental characteristic of the citizen is that he co-operates, in intention if not in fact. Now the man who wishes to cooperate, unless he is one of exceptional powers, will look about for some ready-made purpose with which to co-operate. (p. 11)

I am aware of course that citizenship refers to membership in a state. However, Russell's notion of a citizen applies as well to membership in a work group or corporation. Membership without a distinct and active role is superfluous. And a role implies participation in an enterprise. My experience led me to believe that modern corporations and many governments are vulnerable social systems and will remain vulnerable as long as the individuals are not full citizens. And no individual qualifies as a citizen unless he or she is an integral part of a human

---

[32] Bertrand Russell (1988). *Education and the Social Order*. London: Routledge (first published 1932).

project, which means has a role to play in shaping the future of the institution.

Patients and the Sick Role

The same line of thinking applies to patients in hospitals. Medical treatment involves two parties playing reciprocal roles. Patients have a definite role to play. Becoming sick does not imply total powerlessness. Doctors cannot possibly perform their medical role unless patient also perform the "sick role". Siegler and Osmond (1974) defined the nature of the "sick role."[33] They elucidate the sick role by contrasting it to the *impaired* role:

> The sick role and the impaired role are both called forth by the same events: those situations in which a person can no longer do that which is normally expected of him. But the two roles are very different and in some ways mutually exclusive. In the case of the impaired role, the social pressure serves to aid and maintain normal behavior within the limitations of a given condition, while in the case of the sick role, social pressure serves to discourage normal behavior. Therefore, in terms of function, the two roles are opposites. ... But, unlike the sick person, the impaired person ought to try to do things for himself, and he ought to try to find some useful work. He ought *not* to bother others with every ache and pain. In addition to these differences between the sick role and the impaired role, there are broad differences between the two models.

The difference between the impaired role and the sick role defines the responsibility of the doctor and society towards either the sick or the impaired person. The authors point out:

> ... diagnosis is very important and must be as specific as possible because treatment and prognosis follow from it. In the impaired model, the name of the condition is far more general and tells us what misfortune makes the impaired person different from others: terms such as blind, crippled,

---

[33] Siegler, M. and Osmond, H. (1974). *Models of Madness, Models of Medicine*. New York: Macmillan.

paralyzed, insane, and retarded are used. It is the degree of impairment that is measured, for that will tell what the person will or will not be able to do. Treatment is important in the medical model, even if its efficacy is unknown, for it helps to sustain the person in the sick role and keeps up his hopes. There is no treatment for an impairment, although there may be rehabilitative measures, e.g., if blind, learning to use a Seeing Eye dog. Prognosis in medicine is very important because death is always a possibility and recovery always a hope... In impairment no change is expected, for either better or worse. Hospitals are places where ill people — patients — are treated for their illnesses. Patients *stay* at the hospital, they do not *live* there. They never work *for* the hospital. Institutions for the impaired may serve as protection for the impaired (e.g., colonies for the retarded), protection for the community (e.g., leper colonies), places to live, to work, and to learn reabling skills. (pp. 38, 39)

Siegler and Osmond demonstrate the reciprocal determination of the "sick role" and the "medical role". The sick role applies to both the physically sick and the mentally sick. I must add that the three role components outlined above should be applied to the patient as well as to the doctor. The patient has responsibility and authority within the limits of the medical profession and, of course accountability. With regard to the responsibility or duties of the patient, I had the great fortune of working with Osmond in dealing with schizophrenic patients. Influenced by biographies written by ex-patients, we enlisted schizophrenics' help in developing a diagnostic inventory focusing on the patients' experience of the changes taking place in themselves and in the world around them. Sick as they are, patients are not mentally bankrupt. They can with help from us contribute to the treatment strategy.

Practical Problems and Limitations

Role performance depends on a person's interpretation of the demands of the role relative to identifiable settings. There is often divergence in the way people interpret their own roles and other people's roles. Clarity of role definition on paper minimizes, but does not eliminate, the divergence. Therefore, perfect consensus should not be expected. Nor is it desirable to define a role to the minutest detail lest this would limit flexibility and creativity of the individual worker. Therefore follow-up and constant revision of role definitions must be conducted.

There are several practical dilemmas connected with the implementation of the role concept. One is ambiguity in role perception and imperfection in shared perception of anyone's role. One of the most serious problems in bureaucratic organizations is the tendency towards aggrandizement of authority at the expense of accountability. This is direct reaction to the emphasis on control. Abuse of authority is very likely with the best of intentions.

Role conflict is another problem and it has several variations. For example conflict arises when a person reports to two bosses who make contradictory demands on the same subordinate. Another situation is when the person has the dual role of boss and subordinate, or is a member of the staff and at the same time a representative of the union. A third variation is when the worker's responsibility or authority conflicts with his personal values.

3. Monitoring Membership

The most important implication of the concept of membership is that it should come before leadership. I cannot understand the fact that we focus so much on leadership as a lasting force in the *personality* of a person in a leadership position. The concept of membership must be used as a guide in assessing the mode of existence of an individual in a group or a citizen in a nation. Often deterioration in productivity or morale is a function of alienation, or weakening of the sense of belonging. I met recently with an eminent banker in what was once a great American institution. He explained to me his "ennui":

> The only thing that keeps me in this organization is my clients and my colleagues. My clients are very appreciative of the service we offer. And my colleagues are a bunch of inspiring people. But we are completely isolated from top management by our immediate boss. All she is concerned about is her superiors. And yet she survives thanks to our contributions without acknowledging them. There is so much she can do to

help us produce more but she is rarely available. This resulted in many of my colleagues leaving our organization to the fiercest of our competitors.

This is an example of how membership may decline gradually and suddenly exodus takes place as a big bang. I must point out here that the exodus came about as a result of a boss that defined her membership outside the group she is formally in charge of and relates instead to management through her immediate boss. By so doing, she blocked the subordinates' membership in the institution as a whole. Joining the "enemy camp" was an act of rebellion or revenge.

The concept of membership can serve as a valuable diagnostic tool. Many common problems can be explained in terms of decline or total loss of membership. Suffice it here to mention three that plague bureaucratic organizations — deadwood, corruption, and leadership desertion.

Dead Wood Phenomenon

I often hear from seniors whether in civil service or in the private sector, about the plight they call "dead wood". I usually make two brief comments whenever this issue is brought up to my attention: first, *"no one comes to the organization as a deserter. He or she becomes a deserter in the organization"*. The emphasis is meant to indicate that "dead wood" should be seen as a process that develops in time. It is not an abrupt event that originates in individuals. The organization fails to detect deterioration in performance over time, diagnose it and take corrective action. A seasoned executive once told me, "when I have an important task that has to be done, I look for the busiest guy and assign the task to him." This is certainly an *efficient* action. However, if it becomes the rule rather than the exception, it would translate into reduced investment in long term fostering of quality membership. No living person could be likened to *dead wood*. A more fitting analogy would be a *parasite*. A person taken for "dead" and "wood" is a dynamic force that exerts influence on people about him or her. Even passivity of a person exerts influence on others.

Random House Webster's definition of parasite is: "an organism that lives on or within a plant or animal of another species, from which it obtains nutrients." In an article in *The New York Times* Natalie Anger demonstrates the enormous power of a parasite:[34]

> Most parasites in nature *suck the blood, sip at the gastric juices of the intestines and pierce into the nourishing warmth of muscle tissue. Also, they leech off the fluids and labors of their hosts.* Not only do parasites derive their nutrients from a larger species, but they may alter the behavior of the host. Manfred E. Rau, a parasitologist at McGill University, found two types of closely related parasitic worms that can dramatically influence the behavior of mice to suit their needs. One worm will prompt the mouse to become hyperactive. The mouse gets so agitated that it attracts the attention of a predatory bird that will eat it and the worm with it. When the bird eats the mouse, it gives the next home for the parasitic larvae. By contrast, the related worm species will cause a mouse to become sluggish. This heightens the chance the mouse will be easily stalked down by the carnivorous mammals this worm prefers for its second shelter.

In conclusion, a parasite through living in or on another organism is not a *member*. It is a *foreign* body in active opposition to the host. Incidentally, parasitic existence may characterize leaders as much as followers. We can easily find ample examples of such leaders who are at the helm of either corporate or national institutions. And yet we still call them leaders. We are often deceived by our own metaphors. So here we are confronted once more with the issue of semantics.

Predicting Corruption

Similar analysis may be applied to the phenomenon of corruption. A president of a bank in Indonesia asked me if I could design a psychological test to be applied in recruitment of candidates for the jobs in his organization. He assumed that corruption *resides* in the person as an intrinsic character trait that could be detected by a test. Mind you, that was at the time when Suharto was still President. Corruption

---

[34]Anger, N. (1990, July 17). Parasites take the biological spotlight. *The New York Times.*

was rampant from the head of state down to the first line supervisors. I made it quite clear to the president that corruption is often *learned behavior* and that even if I were able to design the test he hoped for, corruption will not go away. When a problem assumes epidemic proportions it can only be dealt with as a social problem that afflicts the organization as a whole. Conditions in the organization foster the temptation of some to abuse their authority, or take advantage of lax controls for their personal benefit, or abuse the rights of their clients or the public. Often clients participate in corrupting the officials. In the final analysis corruption implies loss of the sense of membership in the organization. It is a form of desertion.

It is wrong to look at corruption as an intrapersonal issue ignoring the conditions that give rise to it as a social phenomenon. Corruption reflects serious organizational failure both as a *social* and a *legal* system. Regarding the former, the system failed to articulate and implement moral values. More seriously, leaders failed to serve as role models. With regard to the latter, the system failed to create and enforce clearly defined rules and regulations. Controls have to be actively enforced. Controls exerted by the boss would not be enough. We should not forget that peers have considerable influence on each other and they would act diligently as controlling force if they have a solid sense of membership in the organization. In the last analysis corruption is the result of weakened membership. Perpetrators of corruption cease to be members the moment they begin to abuse the organization, the client or the public.

Monitoring Leaders' Membership

More important than monitoring membership of the rank and file is monitoring the quality of membership of leaders at all levels of the authority hierarchy. Membership is also the primary force that binds leaders and followers. If we accept the fact that leadership is a mode of exchange between superiors and followers, it becomes necessary to ensure that the relationship is based on common membership. We must ascertain that both parties remain members over time and in a symmetrical manner. Weakening of the sense of membership in either party disrupts role performance of both. Membership should be the primary source of legitimacy of any leader.

Continued identification of the leaders with their respective units should not be taken for granted. Fluctuations of the sense of membership do occur for a variety of reasons. Often remaining in a formal position of leadership for a long time weakens the leader's sense of belonging to the group. Leaders depart from the constituency in various ways. Some leaders who stay long in their position may accumulate dissatisfaction with their constituency to the extent that relationship turns sour. Leaders may then seek solace by siding with certain factions against others in the same constituency. It often happens that leaders seek alliances with outside forces in order to maintain power over their own people. That brings to mind Albert Brecht's biting remark about such leadership, "if a government is dissatisfied with its nation, it should dissolve the nation and elect another one in its place."

Rotation Policy

Rotation sometimes does not provide sufficient time for the manager to establish membership in the new group. And the group would not have enough time to adjust to the newcomer. One of the problems of modern corporations is the mobility of top leaders among organizations. Such leaders scarcely have the time or the inclination to become true members of any organization. Meanwhile members of the organization may see the incoming chairman or president as a stranger. Top leaders of corporations, particularly in the US could be likened to *migratory workers*. Nevertheless they are invested with enormous powers and are usually generously rewarded, sometimes despite their failure.

Status of New Members

One more phenomenon deserves a mention here, namely the status of the young members coming into the organization. A Nobel Prize Laureate has this to say about this issue:

> If we think of education as the primary source of new information, then it is introduced into an organization by its youngest and newest members. Thus we have the possibility of changes in organizational agenda induced by generational changes. More generally, the prime need in organizational

design is increasing capacity to handle a large agenda. To the extent that information and its handling are accumulations of personal capital, what is needed is what Pareto called the "circulation of élites", the turnover of decision-makers. More generally, what is needed is a "circulation of information and decision rules".[35] (p. 59)

I doubt very much if the newest members of the organization are seen in the same light as Kenneth Arrow suggests. In most organizations, newcomers have to spend years before they are considered *experienced* enough to be treated as equal to their seniors. By that time they may have become obsolete, if not *dead wood*. And yet such organizations may claim to be *learning organizations*.

---

[35]Arrow, K. J. (1974). *The Limits of Organization*. New York: W. W. Norton.

Levels of Leading and Following

We can approach either leading or following at different levels: first, as adaptive behavior in dealing with environmental forces; second, as habitual patterns of behavior, and finally as specified social roles. Let us explore each of these three modes one after the other.

1. Leading and Following as Adaptive Behavior

The word "leadership" is too abstract to convey any useful connotation. I do not know what leadership is, but I know it when a person is actually engaged in the act of leading another person, a group or even a flock of sheep. I would also know if the other person, group or the flock of sheep were responding to the leading attempts. Observation of people in daily life shows us that leading and following constitute a feedback system. The act of leading may originate in me but it may also be my response to another person's appeal for my guidance. I may respond to such appeal or decline the quest. If I respond then my leading act may or may not have been an expression of dormant propensity or potentiality.

We do not need more than common sense to see that no human being can survive without readiness both to lead and to follow. Leading here means being ready to take charge sometimes. And this does not exclude the possibility of wanting to depend on others at other times. So what we are talking about here is the adaptive quality of both dependency and independence, or interdependence in short. How else could an infant survive, or a student learn from a teacher, or a patient benefit from a doctor or a citizen comply with a policeman's command? So leading and following coexist as action tendencies that become manifest in response to reality demands. From the standpoint of survival, both leading and following are vital modes of existence *in the world*. I deliberately put emphasis on the phrase "in the world" lest we forget that leadership takes place outside the organism or the psyche.

There are of course many other potentialities that make up the stuff of what we call personality. In fact, personality may be defined as a set of potentialities that unfold in *time* and *place* in response to perceived circumstances. Often, compliance becomes the last resort for survival for any person in captivity. Torture techniques are applied until the captive loses every capacity to maintain his or her autonomy. It is at such point that the captive would have no other choice but depend completely on the captors. Intelligence experts tell us that it will take some time before the captive becomes dependent on his interrogators — for information or for human contact — and begins to provide information that is useful to the captor. This is reminiscent of Freud's observation of the phenomenon of *identification with the aggressor*.

The inverse situation is equally true: a habitually dependent individual may find himself in a situation that forces him to opt for leading even though leading may have been *out of character*. Such is the case when an adult finds himself in the presence of a helpless individual calling for assistance.

2. Leading and Following as Habit Systems

Like any other pattern of behavior, leading may develop into a habitual mode of relating to other people. So we can say that person A is "in the habit of leading" whenever he finds himself in the company of other individuals. In contrast, person B tends to follow other individuals and to seek their guidance. A habit is a consistent pattern of behavior, a trend, a tendency or predisposition. We may go further and state that leading others is typical of person A, whereas following is typical of B. This does not necessarily imply that A will never follow or that B will never lead. Opposites as they are logically speaking, both leading and following attitudes may alternate as patterns of adjustment to social reality. It would therefore be fair to think of leading and following acts in terms of statistical probability. We can say, for example that "A" tends to lead more frequently than he follows. In contrast, B follows more frequently than he leads.

Here we are dealing with leading and following as more or less enduring personality traits, characteristics, or dimensions. The terms "trait", "characteristic" or "dimension" imply continuity and consistency over time, hence predictability. The question may arise as to the reason why A tends to lead more than follows while B tends in the opposite direction. Here we move from describing a phenomenon to explaining it. Explanation may be in terms of a cause, mainly a force that *pushes* (*moves* or *drives*) the individual to act in a certain way. But a person with inquisitive mind would like to explain someone's behavior in terms of the *end or goal* that the actor hopes to attain. The two modes of explanation reflect two opposite movements of the mind. The quest for a cause directs the mind to the past (what happened before). Whereas searching for the goal projects the mind into the future. The former is retroactive while the latter is progressive.

Each trait can be expressed in a variety of ways. A person may lead in an assertive or combative manner. He may also lead in a collegiate or cooperative manner. On the other hand, a person may follow in a meek or submissive way. Alternatively, he may willingly follow in the spirit of trust both in himself and in the person he follows. This means that leading or following does not occur in isolation from other personality dynamics. We must consider, for example, the influence of the person's emotionality and intellectual abilities on the final shape and outcome of either leading or following behavior. We cannot possibly understand leading or following in isolation from the overall psychological context. Nor can we understand either in isolation from the social context. After all, leading or following will always be a mode of relating to other people in an environmental context.

3. Leading and Following as Social Roles

The use of the term *leader* gives the false impression that a member of the organization is either a leader or non-leader. I have yet to find an organization structure that contains special slots for leaders and other slots for followers. Organization structure consists of positions defined in terms of roles, often called job structure. People come into the organization ready to accommodate any authority figure. They were conditioned this way long before they were hired. They do not respond to an authority figure in the abstract, but to a boss in a position imbued with power and status symbols. So there is no separation here between what is intrapersonal or private and what is environmental or public.

As many researchers in social psychology have demonstrated, leadership is both a function of personality and the environment but it is a function of these two in *interaction*. There is no need for additional concept to explain the phenomenon. In fact, there is no justification for saying that "personality qualities which make for leadership exist in latent form when not being exercised in a social situation." (Sherif & Sherif, 1953)

Leadership as a crystallized role does not stem from a specific personality trait. There is nothing within the human personality that we can identify as a discrete trait of leadership. Leadership is a global state of mind, a mode of relating to social situations. Let us suppose that you have been assigned a leadership position. This does not mean that you have become a leader in reality. All you have got at this point is an opportunity to lead. So there is a difference between the event of *ascending* to a position and *acting* according to its requirements. *You become a virtual leader when you engage in leading.* And you do not lead in void. You lead a group of people, members of an institution that transcends both you and them. You enter the history of an organization. Meanwhile you embark on a personal drama, conventionally called career. It is the leading that defines you as a leader. You do not push a button to trigger a discrete personality trait called leadership. You draw on all relevant personal resources — cognitive, affective and even biological. You summon past experiences and call on people for assistance and begin to learn the art of dealing with people. Thus the drama of leadership begins and evolves in time. And it is not only leading that you will be doing. Leading is only one of many facets of your role as a leader. That brings us to the exploration of the other facets to shed more light on the drama of leadership.

Triadic Model of Leadership

In any formal organization, managers have to deal simultaneously with their superiors, subordinates and peers. That means that managers are not, and could not be confined to a leadership mode of existence in all situations. Obvious as it is, this fact is often overlooked in management practices. It is overlooked in selection, placement, training, or performance appraisal. More than a decade ago I presented a model of leadership that takes into account three distinct modes of behavior that any leader has to resort to at different times and in different situations. I referred to this model with the three letters, L-F-F: "Leadership / Fellowship / Followership". (El-Meligi, 1994)[36]

According to this model, people in leadership positions do shift back and forth between three modes of behavior. Thus, I replace the unitary and static conception of leadership by a triadic and dynamic conception. This conception, I believe, reflects the complex and fluctuating reality of leaders' behavior and experience in real life situations.

1. Followership

By *followership* I mean the leader's readiness to put dominance on hold and assume a receptive posture that allows him or her to acquire

[36]An Empirically Derived Leadership / Followership Model. Keynote Address at the Third Afro-Asian Psychological Congress. Kuala Lumpur, Malaysia. August 23–26, 1994.

necessary information or to make use of expert resources. Shifting from a commanding to a receptive attitude is possible only if the leader realizes that power is not infinite and that maintaining control requires an attitude of give and take, negotiation, compromise and changing course. Furthermore, the leader's clarity about accountability enhances his ability to make the shift from commanding to following. In the light of this principle, vulnerability is not always a deficiency. Often it turns out to be a considerable force of influence. It enhances one's influence by gaining trust. Nor should humility be mistaken for weakness.

2. Fellowship

I added a third mode, "Fellowship". This is when a leader suspends the leadership mode to relate to someone who is equal to him or her whether in rank, authority or expertise. Fellowship in this sense provides leaders with additional view of the situation availing them of fresh inputs that otherwise would be missing. Subsequent exploration of the literature showed that my proposition has indeed been confirmed by many people. Take for example Bertrand Russell[37] who noted a long time ago that the separation between leadership and followership on the basis of appearance or formal structure is misleading. Russell states:

> An individual, unable to lead others may content himself with *following* a powerful leader from whom, he hopes, would derive power over others. Or he would content himself with *being equal among equals* in a group and strives with other members to share the triumphs of the group. It is also possible that he would *follow* in the hope to depose the leader or succeed him in future.

Regarding what I call "fellowship", Russell points out that the challenge in organizations is to lead people as equals:

> After anarchy, the natural first step is despotism, because this is facilitated by the instinctive mechanisms of domination

---

[37]Russell, B. (1985). *Power.* London: Unwin paperbacks (first published 1938) [see Chapter 2].

and submission; this has been illustrated in the family, in the State, and in business. *Equal cooperation is much more difficult than despotism*, and much less in line with instinct. When men attempt equal cooperation, it is natural for each to strive for complete mastery, since the submissive impulses are not brought into play. It is almost necessary that all the parties concerned should acknowledge a common loyalty to something outside all of them. In China, family business always succeed because of Confucian loyalty to the family; but impersonal joint-stock companies are apt to prove unworkable, because no one has compelling motive for honesty towards the other shareholders. Where there is government by deliberation there must, for success, be a general respect for law, or for the nation, or for some principle which all parties respect. (pp. 17–18)

There is, however, subtle difference between my proposition and Russell's assertions. I see LFF as three legitimate modes of adapting to social reality. *Fellowship* and *Followership* in my model do not necessarily imply failure in the capacity to lead. On the contrary they may attest to the leader's versatility and flexibility in the use of available resources to meet ever-changing circumstances. These resources would remain idle if the leader were stuck rigidly in a commanding mode or dominated by the illusion of omnipotence. Emil Ludwig (1926) wrote about Napoleon Bonaparte's tendency to relax his dominance and enjoy moments of fellowship in conversing with his staff during the Egyptian campaign:

In the Institute, the commander-in-chief sits as an equal among equals. He never tries, in arguments there, to gain a victory by rank instead of reason. Yet many of the questions that are discussed relate to army matters of immediate practical importance, such as the filtering of Nile water, the erection of windmills, the search for ingredients needed to make gunpowder. On one occasion, Napoleon grew heated. Bertollet said quietly: You are wrong my friend for you have lost your temper. A naval surgeon supported Bertollet. "You men of science are as thick as thieves," exclaimed Bonaparte. "Chemistry plays the cook for medicine, and plays the assassin for science!" The surgeon's answer came out: "But how, Citizen-General, would you define the conqueror's art?"

Napoleon, powerful and dominant that he was, could afford to step out of the clichés of command to enjoy his cultural proclivities. In contrast, Chancellor Bismarck could not easily yield to the expert power of his doctor when the situation of his illness demanded that he does. This is documented in the story of Dr. Schweninger's treatment of Chancellor Bismarck. When Bismarck was sixty-eight, Schweninger was called in for a consultation, and soon confirmed the opinion of the other doctors that Bismarck had not long to live. According to one account:

> ... Schweninger at last imposed moderation on the genius who had imposed it on others, but never on himself. At their first meeting, Bismarck said roughly: "I don't like being asked questions." Schweninger replied: "Then get a vet. He doesn't question his patients." The battle was won in a single round. Bismarck ate and drank less, kept more regular hours. When Schweninger was present, he even kept his temper. He underwent a slimming diet, which consisted exclusively of herrings ... it did the trick. Bismarck's weight went down from eighteen to fourteen stone; he slept long and peacefully; his eyes became clear, his skin fresh and almost youthful.[38] (pp. 94, 95)

It is important to note that Bismarck would not have abandoned his usual dominance had it not been for his doctor's insistence on exercising his expert prerogatives. It is often said that it takes two to tango.

We should differentiate between leadership as a position in a given social system on one hand and leadership as a function on the other. Occupants of leadership positions do not lead all the time nor do they assume a leadership posture with every person they encounter in a given day. In the conduct of their responsibilities, leaders shift between leading and following or between leading and fellowship. They receive guidance as much as they give guidance. They exercise influence but are, at the same time, recipients of influence. The influence they receive may increase or diminish their power depending on their ability to distinguish between what is favorable and what is unfavorable influence.

---

[38]Quoted by Siegler & Osmond (1974).

"Following" does not necessarily imply a defeatist attitude as long as it is a goal-directed act, a voluntary position. The dictionary gives us the following meanings of the word "follow":

> To accept as a guide or leader; to accept the authority of someone else; to conform to, to comply with, or act in accordance with; obey: to follow orders; to follow advice; to move forward along — a road, path, etc. (Random House Webster)

Note that none of the meanings imply weakness, failure or defeat. So it seems that while leading and following are opposites in terms of semantics or logic, they are not so from the existential perspective. In reality, the opposite of leading is either misleading or not leading. Leading and following are two legitimate modes of existence. Alternation between both is necessary for sustaining one's leadership. I might add that the three modes (LFF) ought to be regarded as equally effective patterns of dealing with reality. Each requires its particular sets of skills; and depends on an objective assessment of the situation where it will be deployed. Maintenance of leadership position in the long term calls for flexible and appropriate alternation between the three postures.

Shifting from a leadership posture to a following posture may also occur from a position of weakness such as in the case of asymmetrical power relations. A leader may dominate a powerless party but subordinates himself totally to a more powerful party. This is often the case in failing authoritarian regimes. The authoritarian leader may need the support of a powerful force to enable him to maintain the upper hand over his constituency. Dominance, aggressiveness and autocracy prevail in one relationship while submissiveness, dependency and passivity dominate in a parallel relationship. Certain leaders in Third World Countries consider the zenith of their career an invitation to the White House. Their media celebrate the occasion of their encounters with the US president in an attempt to convince their oppressed people of their leader's international stature. In fact the public knows very well that the leaders go to the White House either to beg for funds, or to reconfirm their control of their peoples or, to receive a new set of orders, or for both ends. I heard many people in a certain Muslim country call the leader's annual visit to Washington the "haj", or pilgrimage to Washington instead of Mecca. People are not really as stupid as some leaders think.

In fact many of the slogans and propaganda in the media of a Third World country are deliberate attempts to get the support of the external master, not the people. The rulers of the Arab world deny the presence of a public opinion in their countries. The only public opinion they recognize is outside their countries, the countries they are supposed to represent. This example sheds light on the prevalence of corruption in some regimes. Often, corruption is a two-way process. The public actively participates in the process, or at least, fuels it by collusion, passivity or indifference.

3. Control versus Influence

The LFF model implies that assessment of a leader's effectiveness in terms of dominance or the ability to control subordinates is insufficient. Readiness to control or dominate has to be supported by appropriate shifting to either a receptive posture or cooperative attitude (fellowship). In the final analysis, the issue is influence. Influence is neither control nor manipulation. It is intriguing that an orchestra conductor is the one to enlighten us as to the shift from power to influence in his career. Herbert von Karajan, the renowned orchestra director tells us:

> You cannot drive orchestras, but you induce them to follow you. I can remember, for example, how Mengelberg conducted quick passages in rehearsal faster than in the performance. Unconsciously the players felt in the concert that they had more time. The bows were longer and the music less driven... *But what I exert over the Berlin Philharmonic is not control, it is influence.* I have worked with them for 20 years. When I first came to the orchestra, I tried to do what so many of my colleagues do — that is to spend only a month or two of the year at home. Then I discovered what I owed my own orchestra, and now I am always there, never away more than two weeks at a time...
>
> If I exert control, it is in rehearsal. When I rehearse, I am like a man with a microscope. I hear everything, every sound. *But in the performance, I let them be free.* At least, they feel

that they are free though they remember the work that has gone on before. When I was young and taking riding lessons, I can remember being afraid of a jump. How I thought, will get this huge animal over the fence? My instructor said to me, 'you must put the horse in the right frame of mind. Then it will carry you over.' This is what I do in conducting."[39] [italics my emphasis]

Interestingly, the analogy of orchestra director was mentioned by one of the most fervent politicians in modern times. This is Lee Kuan Yew, the founder of Singapore. He had this to say about his style in running the government:

> Running a government is not *unlike conducting an orchestra*. No prime minister can achieve much without an able team. While he himself need not be a great player, *he has to know enough of the principal instruments from the violin to the cello to the French horn and the flute*, or he would not know what he can expect from each of them. My style was to appoint the best man I had to be in charge of the most important ministry at that period, usually finance, except at independence, when defence became urgent. That man was Goh Keng Swee. The next best would get the next most important portfolio. I would tell the minister what I wanted him to achieve, and leave him to get on with the task; it was management by objective. It worked best when the minister was resourceful and could innovate when faced with new, unexpected problems. My involvement in their ministries would be only on questions of policy. All the same I had to know enough about their portfolios to intervene from time to time on issues I thought important: a fledgling airline, an airport extension, traffic jams, dispersal of communal enclaves, raising the academic performance of our Malays, and law and order. Some interventions were crucial, and things might have gone wrong had I not intervened. Ultimately, responsibility for a government's failure rests with the prime minister.[40] [italics my emphasis]

---

[39] Quoted by Bertrand Holland in an interview with the conductor.
[40] The Singapore Story from 1965–2000.

The analogy of orchestra conductor places a burden on top leaders, namely to foster leadership potential below their level in the authority hierarchy. Unfortunately this is rarely the case due to the prevalence of the upward stance I referred to earlier as the "boss-oriented" phenomenon. Examples abound of authoritarian leaders who actively suppress lower level leadership. Their onslaught extends beyond the government to destroy existing civil organizations.

Illusions of omnipotence and omniscience in leaders may be at the core of the tendency of some dictators to remain stuck in a controlling position while followers are treated as mentally bankrupt. These illusions tend to be reinforced by the subordinates' failure to exercise the authority invested in their own positions. Such is the case when subordinates fail to provide feedback to the leader out of fear or, worse still, when in the habit to tell the leader what he or she would like to hear.

4. Diffusion of Leadership

Leadership emerges spontaneously parallel to the process of group formation and development. In fact leadership is naturally an integral component of any social role. It is not the exclusive specialty of those assigned the formal roles of leadership. I noted earlier that leadership is a potentiality that may or may not be fully exercised by holders of leadership positions. Fortunately, sound membership in a healthy group will correct for leadership void. We should not leave top leadership isolated so that ultimately they alone receive the accolades of success or suffer the disgrace of failure. Together, all members of an organization ought to assume full responsibility for success and failure. Total dependency on a single leader as the central force in the group weakens leadership as a social force. In a healthy robust culture, people usually volunteer assistance, support, and information to any other member. Pervasiveness of the team spirit as a core value facilitates the diffusion of the leadership function. This is what we mean by public opinion or consensus. We do not wait for a policeman to discover or prevent a crime, we volunteer the information. The older sibling in a family does not wait for parents to warn younger siblings against the dangers of drugs. He or she assumes the role of a senior entitled to direct, discipline, and if necessary, coerce for the sake of the system of which he is a member. Volunteering as a mediator to resolve conflicts or diffuse tension reduces the need to expand the scope of conflict by involving higher levels of authority. A legalistic society or organization depends solely on formal rules and regulation while an informal society relies more on volunteers who assume leadership role when the situations call for it. Finally, I would like to stress that shifting often occurs in a follower from following to leading. Under normal circumstances this happens smoothly and functionally in a healthy group where trust has been established between leaders and followers. Sudden shift may also occur in oppressed followers from compliance to rebellion. That is the topic for the next chapter of the book.

Psychology of Obedience

The tyranny of a prince in an oligarchy is not as dangerous to public welfare as the apathy of a citizen in a democracy.

— Baron De Montesquieu

Every man and woman in democracy should be neither a slave nor a rebel, but a citizen, that is a person who has, and allows to others, a due proportion, but no more, of the government mentality. Where democracy does not exist, the government mentality is that of masters towards dependants; but where there is democracy it is that of equal cooperation, which involves the assertion of one's own opinion up to a certain point, but no further.

— Bertrand Russell in *Power*

1. Varieties of Obedience

The Squirrel and the Snake

Forms of obedience are as varied as forms of leadership. An extreme form of obedience is well illustrated by the phenomenon of the squirrel moving slowly towards the mouth of the snake. The snake does not have to do anything other then fixing its eyes on its victim. Sheer perception of the snake triggers the fatal movement of the squirrel, totally mechanical or biological reaction. This is an extreme form of obedience that dramatizes the passivity of one animal *vis-à-vis* another. Fortunately, there is nothing of this kind of obedience in human interactions except in conditions of stupor or hypnotic trance. Still, the scene symbolizes the degradation of the human person in extreme cases of passive obedience. What I am concerned with here is obedience as a relationship between two parties both of whom are conscious of what is going on between them. What characterizes the relationship in any dyadic structure is power differential. Power is asymmetrical whether we are looking at leading or following. And power differential varies from one dyad to another and in the same dyad from time to time.

We must, however, bear in mind that reversal in the power ratio may occur under certain circumstances and a new power relationship may ensue and persist. The more powerful may lose, or cede the power to the other party while the less powerful may gain the upper hand. Alternation of power positions (between commanding and obeying) may also occur repeatedly and regularly. In other words parties may keep exchanging positions as long as the relationship lasts. This has been noted in relatively enduring relationships — in marriage, in love affairs, or in business partnerships. The alternation follows a detectable rhythm that varies from one dyadic relationship to the other. A pathological variation of this pattern characterizes what is known as sadomasochistic relationships. We may draw two conclusions from this brief introduction, one is that obedience is as much a relationship as is leadership; second, that there are as many variations of obedience as there are of leadership.

Total Dependency

Let us turn our attention to varieties of obedience in human interactions. An extreme form of obedience is characterized by total dependency that may also be sanctioned by the cultural setting of the participants. This type of obedience is not without benefit to the weaker parties. It minimizes the follower's need to strive placing the burden instead on a leader who is willing to shoulder the responsibility. Both parties are locked up in a self-perpetuating feedback system. If obedience is culturally sanctioned, the weaker party sees it fit to comply on moral grounds and the stronger party demands that type of behavior. Since both parties behave in accordance with common norms, there would be no conflict between them.

However the same form of behavior may occur because at some point of the relationship the weaker party *realizes* that compliance is the most prudent or realistic way to relate to a powerful boss. Practicality governs the behavior of the weaker party. Thus peace prevails in the relationship over time. However, the weaker party may experience bouts of sense of inferiority or helplessness. These feelings are soon blotted out or counteracted by expectations of reward. The relationship perseveres along the same line according to norms of utility. All the person has to do is to wait for the master's instructions and carry them out. That is probably the type of employee that is called "dead wood". However, as I said earlier this person would have no chance to survive for long except in an equally "dead wood" organization. Such organization in turn would not be able to survive in a demanding or turbulent environment.

Then we have a follower that consciously and deliberately adopts an obedient posture with more or less concealed resentment. The follower resorts to literal interpretation of the command justifying mechanical implementation of the command and does nothing else pending the next command. In some followers this posture reflects what psychologists call *passive aggressive* attitude. Overtly, the subordinate complies with the boss's demands but finds ways to get back at him or her with impunity. A classical example is to do nothing until he is given instructions. A shrewder pattern would be to resort to literal interpretation of the instructions and implement them accordingly with the knowledge that the outcome will defeat the boss's purpose. There is evidence of creativity in the behavior of apparently passive individuals. But it is self-defeating creativity that perpetuates conflict.

Cynical Obedience

There is still a more active version of obedience for the sake of practical gains. The follower decides to make the most out of a situation where the powerful master controls all rewards besides all means of coercion. This posture is beautifully portrayed by the story of a famous Arab poet who wrote in praise of his strategy:

> Asleep all day, getting drunk at night, and praising the master between the two states of drunkenness; and it is the master that provides for both and it is the poet that delights in both.

This goes on, so the story goes, until the master is replaced by another master, but the poet does not change his ways. Note that in this case obedience afflicts the master himself as he needs other people to support him.

I am not sure if this story were fiction or real. It rings real to me since it represents a universal phenomenon, current and historical. Every dictator surrounds himself with a whole class of people — journalists, intellectuals, experts, politicians, and even courtesans, who follow more or less the Arab poet's cynical strategy. The leader may very well be aware of the true motivation of these people, and may even have contempt for them. Nevertheless, he continues to retain them because he needs them. The relationship is one of mutual exploitation. Expediency characterizes this pattern. Both the leader and the followers in this case may be considered successful entrepreneurs from a purely utilitarian or cynical philosophy of living.

2. Obedience in Bureaucratic Organizations

So far I tried to show that there are various forms of obedience as a prominent feature in a person's behavior or attitude. But obedience like any other personality trait is but one feature in a structure that includes other features. Such features interact dynamically with each other within a global system that we call personality or character. It is not therefore uncommon that dominance and obedience attitudes coalesce in the same person. The issue becomes which is dominant and how they interact with each other in the life of a person. Take for example the structure known as the "authoritarian character". The authoritarian personality is defined by the following constellation of traits according to findings of psychological test designed for that purpose:

1. *Conventionalism*: valuing obedience, respect for authority, and hard work;
2. *Authoritarian submission*: idealizing courageous, tireless and devoted leaders in whom the people can put their trust;
3. *Authoritarian aggression*: abiding by strict discipline, harsh determination and the will to work and fight for the family;
4. *Anti-intellectualism*: valuing business over intellectual or artistic pursuits;

5. *Power and toughness*: power and toughness are supreme values, condemnation of signs of softness or weakness.

The point I meant to stress is that the authoritarianism research concludes that certain individuals have personality needs that include dominance and submissiveness. Research also concludes that authoritarian persons thrive in bureaucratic type of organizations.

Then we come to Whyte's concept of "organization man". The organization man advocates strict adherence to the standards, rules, or demands of the organization. Whyte (1956) argued that American business life had abandoned the old virtues of self-reliance and entrepreneurship in favor of a bureaucratic "social ethic" of loyalty, security, conformity and "belongingness." Whyte's implicit premise was that the change was permanent: that the Organization Man and all he represented would henceforth define the American character. Whyte's work pertains to the era after WWII. More recently however, Virgina Postrel (1999)[41] pointed out that the values observed by Whyte still persist in American business. She observed that young men of ambition "submerged themselves in the organization", adopting what Whyte described as a standard litany: "Be loyal to the company and the company will be loyal to you."

Bertrand Russell (1985) also noted the same phenomenon:

> Among the timid, organisation is promoted, not only by submission to a leader, but by the reassurance which is felt in being one of a crowd who all feel alike. In an enthusiastic public meeting with whose purpose one is in sympathy, there is a sense of exaltation, combined with warmth and safety: the emotion which is shared grows more and more intense until it crowds out all other feelings except an exultant sense of power produced by the multiplication of the ego. Collective excitement is a delicious intoxication in which sanity, humanity, and self-preservation are easily forgotten, and in which atrocious massacres and heroic martyrdom are equally possible. (pp. 19, 20)

---

[41] Postrel, V. (1999). How Has 'The Organization Man' Aged?, *The New York Times*, January 17, 1999.

Russell (1985) makes the analogy of employees in modern enterprises and the slaves in antiquity:

> In an industrial undertaking, there is a distinction analogous to that between citizens and slaves in antiquity. The citizens are those who have invested capital in the undertaking, while the slaves are the employees. I do not wish to press that analogy. The employee differs from the slave in the fact that he is free to change his job if he can, and in his right to spend his non-working hours as he pleases. The analogy that I wish to bring out is in relation to government. Tyrannies, oligarchies, and democracies differed in their relations to free men; in relation to slaves, they are all alike. Similarly in a capitalist industrial enterprise the power may be divided among investors monarchically, oligarchically, or democratically, but employees, unless they are investors, have no share in it whatever, and are thought to have as little claim as slaves were thought to have in antiquity. (pp. 133, 134)

Presthus (1978)[42] helps us to understand how centrality of obedience and loyalty is inherent in the bureaucratic structure of organizations. He writes:

> Hierarchy is perhaps best illustrated by military organization. Ranks and authority are nicely graded from the top to the bottom of the organization. Ideally, this apparatus provides a chain of command extending throughout the entire system, in which each person from commanding general to buck private is under the control of the man immediately above him. At the same time he is himself the supervisor of the person directly below him in the hierarchy. It is not only positions that are ranked in terms of authority, but relative amounts of authority, status, deference, income, and other perquisites of office are ascribed to each position. Such prerequisites [privileges] are allocated disproportionately. They tend to cluster near the top and to decrease rapidly as one descends the hierarchy. This inequitable distribution of scarce values is characteristic of all big organizations; it provides a built-in condition of inequality and invidious [offensive] differentiation. Hierarchical monopoly

---

[42] Presthus, R. (1978). *The Organizational Society*, revised edition. New York: St. Martin's Press.

of the allocative systems augments the power of those at the top since rewards can be assigned so as to reinforce elite definitions of "loyalty", "competence", and so on. A related objective of this inequality is to reinforce the organization's status system, which in turn reinforces the authority and legitimacy of its leaders.

Much of what has been said about dictators, tyrants and despots imply that power is unidirectional — it flows from the powerful to the powerless. This, however, seems to be the end result of a complex process of reciprocal influence. The perpetuation of such aberrations would have been impossible without the readiness of the powerless to accept and tolerate the abuse, and tolerate it for long. This has been noted by philosophers since millennia. David Hume wrote in the *"First Principles of Government"*:

> Nothing appears more surprising to those who consider human affairs with a philosophical eye than the easiness with which the many are governed by the few, and the implicit submission with which men resign their own sentiments and passions to those of their rulers. When we inquire by what means this wonder is affected, we shall find that, as force is always on the side of the governed, the governors have nothing to support them but opinion. It is, therefore, on opinion only that government is founded, and this maxim extends to the most despotic and most military governments as well as to the most free and most popular.

Baron De Montesquieu made a similar remark:

> We should not indulge in blaming the victim. Tyranny of one party and passivity of the other is usually sustained or institutionalized by the overall structure of the organization.

Learned Helplessness

Powerlessness should not be considered as a fate or a condition that springs out of nowhere. It is an end product of a process of learning in which the powerful plays a dominant role. There is a growing body of research about learned helplessness both in animals and human beings. Peterson and his colleagues (1993) stress the generality of learned helplessness among people. They show how learned helplessness gives rise to social problems such as depression and physical health.[43]

Robert Fisk (1993)[44] wrote an insightful article in *The Independent* (London) explaining how authoritarian leaders manage to *infantilize* their people to consolidate their hold on power:

> Many Arab populations have indeed been 'infantilized' by their leaders and regimes. In private, they may cast their eyes to the ceiling to show their abhorrence of the regime, but in front of an audience their enthusiasm might almost be real. And I suspect that it often is real... Because dictatorship does not just bestow brutality and fear upon a society. It takes from the necks of grown people the yoke of blame, the burden of responsibility. They can forget Western adult cares — where to send the children to school, which political party to vote for, how to find the best tax advisor, how to resolve women's rights, equality, crime, social injustice. Under the dictatorship, the people are returned to their childhood. They can live forever as children, forever young, nursed and loved by the Great Father, the Caliph, the Sultan, he whom God has chosen to protect them and guide them, a guide who has only to look into his own heart to know what his people think ...

Speer (1995)[45] wrote in his memoirs describing his experience under the influence of Hitler:

> Under normal circumstances a fall from the heights of power might be attended by grave inner crises. But to my astonishment the fall took place without any perceptible turmoil. I also adapted quickly to the conditions of imprisonment. I ascribe that to my twelve years of *training in subordination.* For in my own mind I had already been a prisoner under Hitler's regime. Relieved at last of the responsibility for daily decisions, I was overpowered during the early months by a craving for sleep such as I have never felt before. A slackening of the mind took place, although I tried not to let it show.

---

[43] Peterson, C., Maier, S. F. and Seligman, M. E. P. (1993). *Learned Helplessness: A Theory for the Age of Personal Control.* New York: Oxford University Press.

[44] Robert Fisk, "Iraq: A Year of War". *The Independent*, 17 March 2004.

[45] Speer, A. (1995). *Inside the Third Reich: Memoirs.* New York: Galahad Books, pp. 500–501.

With the disappearance or weakening of self-regard, the person is ready to lose himself in a stranger's ego. Once a person has accepted his slavery, he ceases to live his own life. His life is not his anymore, it belongs to someone else. Malcolm X differentiated between the house Negro and the plant Negro. When the master gets sick the house negro would ask, "me sick master?"

Étienne de la Boétie (1530–1563) wrote a thesis about obedience to tyrants under the title "Servitude volontaire", voluntary servitude or slavery. He was puzzled by the fact that thousands of individuals, towns and whole nations surrender their freedom to a tyrant and serve him without questioning or rebellion. He starts out from the premise that love of freedom is inherent in nature, that animals of all kinds fight to death to defend their freedom. The desire to remain free arouses the little intelligence an animal possesses to defend its freedom. Animals resist capture and put up a fight using nails, corns, beak and feet and when they cannot fight any more they give us ample signs that they are aware of their misery and that they would rather die than live in slavery. La Boétie gives the example of the elephant that defends its freedom until it has no more force left, at which point it sticks its jaws and breaks its teeth against the tree. It is as if the elephant threatened by loss of its freedom is willing to give up its ivory in exchange for freedom.[46]

La Boétie[47] observes that the animals we domesticate would not accept servitude without showing some form of protest. De la Boetie was preoccupied with the dilemma that man who is the only creature who is truly born to lead a free life and yet when he loses his freedom he loses the memory of his earlier freedom and the desire to regain it. La Boétie wonders how hundreds or thousands of human beings, even whole nations surrender to the tyranny of a single person. Love of freedom is intrinsic in nature. People are not only born free but they are also born with the readiness to defend their freedom and fight to maintain it and struggle to regain it when they lose it. Why then do we see thousands of human beings, even whole towns and entire

---

[46]I am grateful to Professor Mustapha Safwan, the French Egyptian psychoanalyst for drawing my attention to De la Boétie's work.

[47]De la Boétie, É. (1983). *Discours de la servitude volontaire*. [A treatise on voluntary slavery]. Paris: Flammarion. (First published 1574.)

nations lose their freedom to a single tyrant and willingly accept to lead their life in servitude for him? Even cowardice would not be sufficient to explain this horrendous misery. Says la Boétie, "When a nation that was defeated and finally surrender to a victorious tyrant, the nation sinks in a state of forgetfulness of its own freedom to the extent that it becomes unable to wake up and regain it. Instead the nation would rush to serve the tyrant who deprived them of freedom. They behave as if they have *gained servitude* rather than *having lost* their freedom." He then says that it may be true that initially people may not seek to serve the tyrant except under duress. However, those who come after them serve without any regret and do willingly what their predecessors had accepted to do by necessity. They accept the conditions of their birth as a fate and do not think otherwise. De la Boétie concludes:

> The primary reason why men give in for voluntary servitude is the fact that they were born serfs and brought up as such. This leads to the second reason which is that under a tyrant it is easy for people to become cowards and effeminate. (p. 153, my translation)

Function of Rebellion

We cannot depart from the subject of obedience without mentioning the phenomenon of rebelliousness as a reaction to long submission to excessive dominance.

Bertrand Russell

Russell (1985) concludes the chapter on morality by a statement about the function of rebellion:

> Without rebellion, mankind would stagnate, and injustice would be irremediable. The man who refuses to obey authority has, therefore, in certain circumstances, a legitimate function, provided his disobedience has motives which are social rather than personal. But the matter is one as to which, by its very nature, it is impossible to lay down rules. (p. 172)

In his book on *Power* (1995) Russell expounds on the psychological conditions for the taming of power:

The psychological conditions for the taming of power are in some ways the most difficult. In connection with the psychology of power we saw that fear, rage, and all kinds of violent collective excitement, tend to make men blindly follow a leader who, in most cases, takes advantage of their trust to establish himself as a tyrant. It is therefore important, if democracy is to be preserved, both to avoid the circumstances that produce general excitement, and to educate in such a way that the population shall be little prone to moods of this sort. Where a spirit of ferocious dogmatism prevails, any opinion with which men disagree is liable to provoke a breach of the peace. Schoolboys are apt to ill-treat a boy whose opinions are in any way odd, and many grown men have not got beyond the mental age of schoolboys. A diffused liberal sentiment, tinged with scepticism, makes social cooperation much less difficult, and liberty correspondingly more possible. (pp. 200, 201)

Albert Camus

Albert Camus conceives rebellion as an *act* and offers in-depth analysis of this act in his book *Le Revolté*[48]. He defines a rebel in the following passage:

> [A rebel] is a person that says NO. But while refusing he does not give up: he is also a person that says yes, from the very first move. A slave who had received orders all his life, suddenly decides that a new command is unacceptable. What is the meaning of this "no"?
>
> It means that "things have lasted too long", "heretofore yes, from now on it will be "no", "you went too far", moreover, "there is a limit you cannot go beyond". In short, this "no" affirms the existence of a boundary. We find the same notion of boundary in the rebel's feeling that the other "exaggerates", that he stretches his right beyond the boundary where the right of someone else confronts and stops him. Therefore, the act of rebellion rests on a categorical rejection of intrusion that the rebel judges to be intolerable and on a vague belief in a right, or to be more exact, the rebel's impression that

---

[48] Camus, A. (1951). *L'homme revolté*. Paris: Gallimard.

"he is entitled to ... "There is no rebellion without the conviction that somehow one is right." That is how the rebel slave says yes and no simultaneously. Besides affirming the existence of boundary, he also affirms whatever he suspects and wishes to preserve on his side of the boundary. He demonstrates stubbornly that there is something in him that is "worth...", something that must be recognized." It is as if the rebel has found something in himself to identify with, something he values more than himself, even more than life itself. (p. 25, my translation)

Saying "no" implies that at last the rebel has found within himself something to hold on to, to identify with and defend tenaciously. Camus explains how saying "no" marks the end of despair:

He kept silent, to say the least, surrendering to despair of a condition despite knowing it to be unjust. Being silent gives the impression that one neither judges nor wants anything. In some cases not wanting anything is true. However, despair, like the absurd, judges, and wants everything in general, and nothing in particular, Silence spells that out. But the moment the person speaks, even just saying no, he desires and judges. [At that moment] the rebel makes a full turn around, literally speaking. After years of marching to the lashes of the whip, the slave turns around and faces the master." (p. 26, my translation)

Camus adds that the moment the rebel refuses to carry out a command he *judges* to be demeaning he, for the first time, faces the master as adversary. In fact, states Camus, the command that gave rise to "no" may have been less repugnant than any of the past injustices the rebel had long tolerated. This implies that "no" does not only refute the latest command, but at the same time, refutes all past injustices. Indeed he refutes slavery itself.

Thus Camus puts rebellion in a historical context. Rebellion is not a simple *response* to a current *stimulus* as a Skinnerian psychologist would put it. Rather, it is a global act implying that the rebel has grasped the entire tragedy of slavery. In addition to historical awareness, the act of rebellion gives rise to "sudden and vivid perception" that there is something within the rebel to identify with and to defend tenaciously. This awareness the rebel values more than himself and even more than life itself. For him it becomes the supreme good. He may have compromised in the past but his position now is ALL or NONE. Such is the state of mind that ensues directly from the act of rebellion. The new state of mind is what could be called *freedom*, "Better die than live kneeling down."

The rebel's attitude of ALL or NONE proves that the act of rebellion, counter to the current opinion, is not strictly individualistic. In the first place, rebellion does not originate only in the oppressed. It may also originate in a person who happened to witness the oppression of others. This comes about through identification with the oppressed. But it is not the usual psychological mechanism, a subterfuge according to which the witness imagines himself to be the oppressed person — in fact we may feel oppression inflicted upon our enemies to be equally repugnant — quite on the contrary, this may happen because:

> [The witness] could not bear seeing offences inflicted upon other people, that we ourselves had suffered without daring to rebel … In rebellion man passes over to the other and, from this point of view, human solidarity is metaphysical. The issue at this point is simply nothing but the solidarity that was born in chains. (p. 29)

Camus adds the affirmation implicit in the act of rebellion extends to something that surpasses what is strictly individual and connects the rebel to other people. They also are entitled to the same right. To the rebel, the issue is no more himself but all the oppressed of the world.

Camus refutes the explanation of the rebel's humanitarianism in terms of *commonality of interests* with other oppressed people. Says Camus, "Man's passion for man does not necessarily come about as a result of arithmetic calculation of interests, nor as a result of theoretical belief in human nature." (p. 31)

Camus also points out that rebelling transcends revenge. It is more than an attempt to get even or to settle scores of the past otherwise it would be a form of "auto-intoxication". Rebellion puts an end to stagnation and liberates hemmed-in energies.

Leadership Prerequisites

There is no such thing as a perfect leader either in the past or present, in China or elsewhere. If there is one, he is only pretending, like a pig inserting scallions into its nose in an effort to look like an elephant.

— Liu Shao-chi (b. 1898)[49]

The love of power is a part of normal human nature, but power-philosophies are, in a certain precise sense, insane. The existence of the external world, both that of matter and that of other human beings, is a datum, which may be humiliating to a certain kind of pride, but can only be denied by a madman. Men who allow their love of power to give them a distorted view of the world are to be found in every asylum...

— Bertrand Russell in *Power*

1. Meaning of "Prerequisite"

Here I must start by defining the term "prerequisites". According to the dictionary, prerequisite means, "Something required beforehand, mandatory, essential, *sine qua non*, (French: de rigueur) indispensable or essential characteristics that are precondition for any other attribute."

---

[49] Quoted in: Stanley Karnow, *Mao and China: From Revolution to Revolution*, Ch. 4 (1972).

In the course of teaching students or lecturing to managers, I made it a policy to ask participants to identify the characteristics of the type of leader they would like to work for and be willing to follow. I would then project the list of the attributes on a screen, and invite comments thus initiating a discussion about criteria of effective leadership. I did that several times in the US and Europe. Later on, I repeated the same exercise in Malaysia. Participants in the seminar were senior government officials. They were Muslims. I projected the list they produced on the screen and posed the question: Does any one of you have ever encountered a leader that has all these attributes. Because participants were Muslims and I gathered beforehand what the answer would be because I too am Muslim. The answer came as I had expected: "only God the Almighty".

At a later stage, I resorted to a more modest request, asking participants to identify only the three qualities of the best boss they would like to work for. The list turned out to be both realistic and more manageable. Inspection of the list I collected from several groups yielded a meaningful classification to a limited number of attributes. However, I did not wait for statistical tallying of the resulting attributes. I concluded after years of observation and interface with leaders that five basic conditions have to be met before the person can embark on a leadership career. I postulated that no leadership potential or leadership quality could work unless these prerequisites are met. The prerequisites, I believe, transcend cultures and correct for the limited applicability of Western models of leadership in Asian cultures. Actually I started out with four prerequisites and it was not until later that I realized that a fifth prerequisite comes so often that I decided to add it to the original four.

These five attributes constitute a common denominator to any presumed style of leadership and without which no leadership qualities can be put to good use. In this section I will present the model I developed in the course of my studies and contacts in both Western and Asian countries. The model takes into consideration the cultural and situational diversity. I will not offer universal criteria of effective leadership. Instead I will highlight five universal prerequisites that have to be met by any normative model.

1. The will to lead (motivational dimension)
2. Clarity (cognitive state of mind)
3. Similar and yet different (social role)
4. Ability to learn (developmental dimension)
5. Energy resources (psychobiological dimension)

2. The Will to Lead

Meaning of "Will"

Many of the older views of the concept of *will* stressed the inhibiting function of the will. According to these views, will is a force that inhibits activity. Still others regard it as a force *pushing* the person to act. Fortunately, the concept of will is gradually finding its way back into modern psychology after a period of banishment. In the humanistic approach, sometimes called the "third force" in modern psychology, the concept of will is accorded a central place within the psyche; being seen as a direct expression of the Self. A true act of will, on the higher levels, is an integral act which involves commitment of the whole person to a goal which is both realistic and worthwhile; such an act mobilizes energies of vast power. Gordon Allport (1960) points out that theories of motivation use concepts which refer exclusively to the past and stresses the need for concepts which refer to man's future. He finds it necessary to stress the forward *thrusts* of motivation that are so characteristic of human personality, thrusts that "cannot adequately be accounted for by any doctrine of *pushes*, even a sequence of pushes, out of the past".

An adequate theory, says Allport, "must allow for the effectiveness of a current self-image and for the dynamic character of intentions, of value-orientations and of uniquely patterned psychogenic interest systems in normally healthy adults." (page 28) Will as I understand it is not a *push*, or a *thrust*, or *compulsive* act. Rather it is a choice and steady movement forward. The movement is consciously and voluntarily undertaken by the person as a whole entity towards a goal the person considers important to reach. In view of this definition, I must point out there is a significant difference between *wanting* to lead and *needing* the position or status associated with leadership.

To Lead or Not to Lead

Highly specialized experts are beginning to crowd the upper echelons of the authority hierarchy. More and more of them are called upon to assume leadership responsibilities. This is a distinctive feature of our times. Some of these people would rather remain in their professional niches to deliver the expertise they were trained to deliver. And yet as technocrats they are inevitably required to lead masses of people. It is prudent to anticipate that at least a sizeable minority of these people will accept the leadership responsibilities under duress.

Some managers I knew were forced into leadership positions. Initially, they functioned below expectation. Unless they reconcile themselves with the leading aspects of their managerial role, they will go through the motion with minimum of job satisfaction. Some, however, manage to pull through and acquire a taste for the job. And it is only then that they began to capitalize upon untapped inner resources. A dramatic improvement in their performance took place as a result.

Initially, the dilemma these people have to resolve is: "to lead or not to lead". They will have to make a choice. Once they have accepted the mandate wholeheartedly, personal resources are mobilized. To many of such experts, shedding the ambivalence they harbored heretofore was all that is needed to engage in the business of leading. I have seen this happening to first class scientists in R&D units of several firms. Thus the will to lead must be a direct expression of the *Self*, the innermost essence within the person. A true act of will at that level is an integrated movement, total commitment to a goal. It channels energies in the pursuit of a goal unimpeded by complexes or contradictions.

Complexity of the Will to Lead

The will to lead derives from diverse motivational sources and finds expression in a wide range of activities. Different leaders draw on different motivational sources and are guided by different value orientations. The will to lead is a complex sentiment in which we can discern several interdependent components: first, it is a movement into the world, away from one's inner world; second, it implies readiness to assume responsibility for others; third, willingness to exercise the authority invested in the leadership role, and finally acceptance of accountability to higher authority or a constituency.

The will to lead is subject to contradictions: the contradiction between performing as an expert and discharging the many tasks of management. There is also the issue of double membership in the group assigned to the leader and the entire organization — how to reconcile his commitment to the organization and the demands of the immediate group. There is still another source of conflict at a deeper psychological level between dominance and fellowship.

Fluidity of the Will to Lead

The will to lead is subject to fluctuations depending on the leader's mood changes and the followers' receptivity. Leaders may harbor hostile feelings towards followers who, in their perception, have failed them. Often such feelings find their way to hostile expression. An extreme example is Hitler's decision to drown Berlin underground and blaming the defeat on his generals. It is very helpful if the leader has immunity to hostile reactions or demonstrates ability to survive rejection or any manifestation of hostility.

Leaders vary with regard to the degree of effectiveness in the way they integrate themselves into the group and the speed with which they start leading. Initially, they rely maximally on their inner resources rather than on situational demands. Others become effective leaders, after having gained some experience.

Degeneration of the Will to Lead

What appears to be an active will to lead may be in reality egocentric need to get others to do things that one decides are worth doing. It is then that *The Will to Lead* may degenerate into efforts for self glorification or for intimacy. The former generates tyranny, the latter dependency. In either case the authority of the leader suffers. A tyrant, the young Thomas More wrote, "is a man who allows his people no freedom, who is puffed up by pride, driven by the lust of power, impelled by greed, provoked by thirst for fame". The will to lead should rule out addiction to power. Most pervasive and corrosive corruption is where leadership position becomes a means to self enrichment.

Another form of degeneration is addiction to power. It is expressed in the refusal to share power or passing it over to a trusted nobody or to a son. The latter case has become endemic in authoritarian regimes in Third World countries. Examples are in Syria and Egypt in what has become to be known as the issue of inheritance. Another manifestation of degeneration of the will to lead is a split in the will into two opposing behavior tendencies. Leaders then would behave towards their subordinates as ferocious tigers and towards their superiors as compliant lambs. Here we find a pathological split between the will to lead and the will to ingratiate. Finally there is the phenomenon of excessive dependency on experts (spin doctors), on technology, on favored subordinates, or being fixated on past achievements. The central core of the will to lead is implicit in the word *lead*. A leader is supposed to lead, not to mislead. This sounds too naïve, unscientific, or too obvious. However the point should always be reiterated. And misleading comes in various forms: lying, deceiving, or what is equally reprehensible, seducing.

3. Clarity

Definition

Getting away from the motivational sphere to the cognitive level of functioning, we must take note that exercise of leadership must first engage the cognitive processes of the leader — the processes of perception, imagination, assessment and analysis. These processes work in a harmonious fashion to the extent that the mind is clear. Clarity is not a state one achieves once for all. It is not a finite act. It is a mode of existence that develops as a result of dealing with events as they occur in daily life. Achieving clarity is the greatest challenge a leader encounters in his / her career as a leader.

Clarity can never be a purely subjective matter. It cannot be achieved simply by introspection. It is not clarity about oneself in isolation from the external circumstances which are often muddled and ambiguous. The ability to reflect is of course involved in the process. However, reflection will not be forthcoming unless the person is able to delay action. Delay of action, no matter how brief, allows the person to orient himself prior to action.

But reflection is not absolute rationality. Highly rational individuals, especially those who avoid their own feelings, get disoriented if their emotions get the best of them. Intellect as Bertrand Russell has stated, "may guide and direct, but does not generate the force that leads to action. The force must be derived from emotions. Emotions that have desirable social consequences are not so easily generated as hate and rage and fear." (Russell, in *Power*, p. 205)

Clarity does not occur in a linear or uniform fashion. Often it springs up as an intuitive leap. This is not to say that it springs from nowhere. Long preoccupation with, and interest in an issue precedes what appears to be a sudden insight. We should not confound clarity of mind with intelligence. This is because reflection occurs at all levels of intelligence. I refer here to the concept of intelligence as measured by IQ tests. IQ is a statistically derived measure of probability or potentiality rather than actuality. Unfortunately an intelligent person does not always live up to his or her intellectual potential. In fact, when a highly intelligent person commits a mistake it is usually at the level of that person's intellectual endowment. Something more than IQ is required. This something is sound judgment. The most important component in judgment is emotional awareness and emotional control.

Finally, to be convinced does not mean to become clear. Clarity must come as a result of questioning. You would not question if you were certain. Descartes based his entire philosophical system on methodical doubt.

Clarity and Relevance

Clarity is not commensurate to the volume of knowledge. In fact, too much knowledge causes overload. Experientially, overload is always associated with confusion or intellectual disorientation. It has the effect of either delaying action or causing indecision. What is really needed is relevant information. But what exactly do we mean by relevance? The dictionary offers two meanings: first, bearing upon or connected with the matter at hand; second, having practical value or applicability. One must go one step further beyond the registration of events and explore what events mean, what they imply. Reality testing is not passive reception of objective facts. It implies intention to see and courage to select what aids action in a given situation. As such, *intention* is a form of assertiveness though at a cognitive level.

What a leader needs is the ability, and indeed the courage, to simplify rather than accumulate knowledge beyond what is needed. One of the great assets attributed to Field Marshall Montgomery is *simplification of the complicated*. Roland Lewin (1971) made several references to this asset in his biography of Field Marshall Montgomery:

> Indeed, he elevated simplification of the complicated into a high art. I have talked to many senior officers (not, by any means, all his admirers) and over and over again the point was stressed by his comrades-in-arms that he had a particular gift for reducing an abstruse military problem to the basic and communicable essentials. This is no mean ability in a representative of a type often considered inarticulate and unsophisticated. There is sophistication in simplification — if it entails a reduction of muddle to clear and comprehensible truths... (p. 24)

It was an axiom for Montgomery that clarity and simplicity cannot be achieved by a mind muddled with a plethora of minor detail ... It was whole woods that Montgomery was mainly interested in. Lewin goes on to explain the essence of Montgomery's "perennial search for clarity and simplicity":

> He believed, in effect, that every problem has a heart and that if you can penetrate to the very heart the resolution of the problem will present no difficulty. He sought always to probe to the essence of a matter, with a mind like a laser beam. Having found the essence, he could then define it to himself and so to others in crisp, brief and unusually simple terms. (p. 51)

Clarity and Common Sense

When talking about clarity we should bear in mind that cognition includes sense perception. The Latin saying *Veritas est adaequatio intellectus et rei* (truth consists in the agreement of thought with reality). Sensory input into the thought process is conducive to clear thought. Neglect of the banal in favor of intellectualization is a mark of elitism that is condemned by deep thinkers. Wittgenstein, one of the greatest minds in modern times goes as far as advising: "don't think, just look". He meant to warn us against rushing into dialectic without being clear about what we are talking about.

Another modern philosopher, Susan Langer (1974)[50] joins in to stress the role of "seeing" in intellectual activity:

> The nervous system is the organ of the mind; its center is the brain, its extremities the sense organs; and any characteristic function it may possess must govern the work of all its parts. In other words, the activity of our senses is "mental" not only when it reaches the brain, but in its very inception, whenever the alien world outside impinges on the furthest and smaller receptor. All sensitivity bears the stamp of mentality. "Seeing," for instance, is not a passive process, by which meaningless impressions are stored up for the use of an organizing mind, which construes forms out of these amorphous data to suit its own purposes. *"Seeing" is itself a process of formulation; our understanding of the visible world begins in the eye.* (p. 90)

Non-intellective factors have to be considered in approaching clarity. If we do that, we come much closer to the common notion of wisdom. Wisdom according to Russell (1985) is not merely intellectual. In his book on *Power* Russell asserts:

> But wisdom is not merely intellectual, intellect may guide and direct, but does not generate the force that leads to action. The force must be derived from the emotions. Emotions that have desirable social consequences are not so easily generated as hate and rage and fear. In their creation, much depends upon circumstances. Something, however, can be done, in the course of ordinary education, to provide the nourishment upon which the better emotions can grow, and to bring about the realisation of what may give value to human life. (p. 205)

We must then add Bergson's contribution to the theory of knowledge. Bergson expanded the scope of intellectual activity to include intuition

---

[50]*Philosophy in a New Key: A Study in the Symbolism of Reason, Rite, and Art* (third edition). Cambridge, Mass.: Harvard University Press.

and sympathy. In his volume on "creative evolution" Bergson[51] had this
to say:

> But, in default of knowledge properly so called, reserved
> to pure intelligence, intuition may enable us to grasp what
> it is that intelligence fails to give us, and indicate the means
> of supplementing it. On the one hand, it will utilize the
> mechanism of intelligence itself to show how intellectual molds
> cease to be strictly applicable; and on the other hand, by its own
> work, it will suggest to us the vague feeling, if nothing more, of
> what must take the place of intellectual molds. Thus, intuition
> may bring the intellect to recognize that life does not quite go
> into the category of the many nor yet into that of the one; that
> neither mechanical causality nor finality can give a sufficient
> interpretation of the vital process. Then, by the sympathetic
> communication which it establishes between us and the rest
> of the living, by the expansion of our consciousness which it
> brings about, it introduces us into life's own domain, which is
> reciprocal interpenetration, endlessly continued creation. But,
> though it thereby transcends intelligence, it is from intelligence
> that has come the push that has made it rise to the point it has
> reached. (pp. 177, 178)

We can see how right Tolstoy has been when he condemned pure
intellect: "The more we live by our intellect, the less we understand the
meaning of life."[52]

4. Imparting Clarity[53]

Clarity has two sides to it, the intrapersonal and the interpersonal. You
may be clear about your ideas but fail to impart clarity to others. You
as a leader may have a vision that is so luminous in your mind, but fail
to impart the experience to other people. Meanwhile, your vision may
have been the end product of your subjective experience. As long as

---

[51] Bergson, H. (1998). *Creative Evolution.* transl. A. Michell. Mineola, NY: Dover
Publications.
[52] Quoted by William Barrett, p. 35.
[53] Blair has been accused of being the "real misleader", "culture of deceit" has "poisoned
the whole of politics", with Mr. Campbell acting as his loyal assistant.

you are in the business of leading, the issue will always be imparting clarity. This will be possible if you entertain a measure of doubt in your own convictions. Doubt implies readiness to test your perceptions against other peoples' perception. This is what psychologists call *consensual validation*.

In *The Art of War*, Sun Tzu stresses the ability of imparting clarity as vital leadership attribute. He says:

> If words of command are not clear and distinct, if orders are not thoroughly understood, the general is to blame. But if his orders are clear and the soldiers nevertheless disobey, then it is the fault of their officers.[54]

Napoleon was equally emphatic about the same issue:

> The first qualification in a general in chief is a cool head that is, a head which receives just impressions, and, estimates things and objects at their real value. He must not allow himself to be elated by good news, or depressed by bad. The impressions he receives, either successively or simultaneously in the course of the day, should be so classed as to take up only the exact place in his mind which they deserve to occupy, since it is upon a just comparison and consideration of the weight due to different impressions that the power of reasoning and of right judgment depends. Some men are physically and morally constituted as to see everything through a highly coloured medium. They raise up a picture in the mind on every slight occasion, and give to every trivial occurrence a dramatic interest. But whatever knowledge, or talent, or courage, or other good qualities such men may possess, nature has not formed them for the command of armies, or the direction of great military operations. (Chandler, 1988, p. 80)

---

[54] Sun Tzu (1993). *The Art of War*. In J. Clavel (ed.). New York: Delta. (First published 1910, p. 4.)

The Principle of Specificity

I must stress at this juncture that clarity is not a general attribute that covers all situations. A leader cannot say, "I am generally clear," but should approach every specific situation as a new situation worthy of inspection. Clarity should be viewed as the habit of posing a simple question: "Am I clear?" Going into a meeting, for example, you would ask yourself: "Why am I here?", "What is my role?", "What am I expected to offer?", "What can I contribute?" Admission of uncertainty or of ignorance is a supreme indicator of clarity — "I don't know, therefore I must find out." Short term is of the essence in developing clarity as a way of life. Leader's perception of situational parameters was found to be more predictive of person-situation match than were objective assessments of those variables. In other words how structured the leader perceived a task to be or how supportive subordinates were seen to be was a better predictor than were the objective nature of the task or the actual reports of those subordinates.

Clarity about What

The question that arises now is what should the leader be clear about?

First and foremost is the leader's clarity about the constituency of which he is a member. But the constituency does not exist in void. It is entangled in a web of other constituencies. To put it more specifically, the leader's primary task is the delineation of the boundary of his constituency and its field of action.

Second, the leader must be clear about his role. A role by definition is a *relational* notion. It follows that the leader must be clear about role interdependencies. The issue is not power in the abstract or power *generally speaking*, but legitimate power relative to a specific constituency. Furthermore it is power as a means to accomplish the tasks assigned to the leader by certain legitimate authority. The best form of assertiveness takes place at the mental level it is the courage to exercise self definition. There are many possible definitions: manager; steward; custodian; teacher; public servant; supervisor; overseer; and many other possible definitions.

Third, a role should be clearly aligned with the mission of the global social system within which the leader performs the role. I have witnessed many leaders whose concern with organization mission ended with the articulation of a mission statement. Mission statement becomes an end in itself. It is on paper. What the mission is supposed to do is to provide guidance and guarantee coherence in setting up the agenda the leader wishes to implement throughout his or her tenure. I must stress at this point that a role is time-bound. The leader must be clear about the timeframe as a property of the role. Effectiveness in any role cannot be assessed except in relation to the timeframe within which the role will be deployed.

Fourth, a leader must be clear about his or her value system and the value implications of the organization's mission. This is mandatory because values are involved in the selection of problems one must grapple with and in the key conceptions one uses in the formulation of these problems. Finally, values affect the course one will ultimately take for their solution. A leader must have a clear idea about how far he can go in making compromises without jeopardizing his authority or his credibility.

William James in *Selected Papers on Philosophy* sees truth as a prerequisite for clear thinking: "Truth must bring clear thoughts, as well as clear the way for action." (p. 223) James finds it impossible "to inspire clarity while issuing falsehood, duplicity or misrepresentation... Double-dealing enhances uncertainty and skepticism in the minds of the constituency." However, abiding consistently by one's values is not a simple matter. Contradictions often characterize one's value system. That adds a burden the leader must tackle. In the first place, he must unravel such contradictions and attempt to resolve them.

C. Wright Mills has this to say about this issue:[55]

> But when there are values so firmly and so consistently held by genuinely conflicting interests that the conflict cannot be resolved by logical analysis and factual investigation then the role of reason in that human affair seems at an end. We can clarify the meaning and the consequences of values, we can make them consistent with one another and ascertain their actual priorities, we can surround them with fact — but in the end we may be reduced to mere assertion and counter-assertion;

---

[55] Mills, C. Wright (1959). *The Sociological Imagination*. London: Oxford University Press.

then we can only plead or persuade. And at the very end, if the end is reached, moral problems become problems of power, and in the last resort, if the last resort is reached the final form of power is coercion. (p. 77)

5. Ability to Learn

Learning Develops in Time

Leadership does not spring into existence in a sudden way. It is not an event in time to be explained by a pre-existing propensity within the leader's psyche. It is a historical process. It emerges in time and a place that brings the leader in contact with other people we call subordinates or followers. There is a lot of learning that takes place, or should take place by the leader during his or her tenure.

The ability to learn presupposes willing to learn. Some leaders stop learning when they reach a certain level of confidence engendered by success. Success and admiration it brings about may obviate the need for further learning. After initial period of success, a leader may reach the point of believing that he "knows it all". Obsolescence sets in along with decline of expert power. By learning here I mean learning the job of leading, not learning in general. Napoleon stressed that the leader must learn from his experience:

> Generals in chief must be guided by their own experience or their genius. Tactics, evolutions, the duties and knowledge of an engineer or an artillery officer may be learned in treatises, but the science of strategy is only to be acquired by experience, and by studying the campaigns of all the great captains.[56]

Error is the Main Source of Learning

The most effective source of learning in the job of leading is the errors the leader makes. It follows that fear of making errors inhibits learning and ends by stagnation. Denial of errors is another inhibiting force. But what kinds of errors do a leader learn from? They are not necessarily the big mistakes. Popper points out that we cannot learn

---

[56]Quoted by Chandler, 1988, p. 81.

from big mistakes.[57] Popper is very critical of the view that we can learn from *holistic experiments* or from measures carried out on a scale that approaches the holistic dream:

> ... Our main point is very simple: it is difficult enough to be critical of our own mistakes, but it must be nearly impossible for us to persist in a critical attitude towards those of our actions which involve the lives of many men. To put it differently, it is very hard to learn from very big mistakes. The reasons for this are twofold; they are technical as well as moral. Since so much is done at a time, it is not possible to say which particular measure is responsible for any of the results; or rather, if we do attribute a certain result to a certain measure, then we can do so only on the basis of some theoretical knowledge gained previously, and not from the holistic experiment in question. This experiment does not help us to attribute particular results to particular measures; all we can do is to attribute the 'whole result' to it; and whatever this may mean, it is certainly difficult to assess. Even the greatest efforts to secure a well-informed, independent, and critical statement of these results are unlikely to prove successful. But the chances that such efforts will be made are negligible; on the contrary, there is every likelihood that free discussion about the holistic plan and its consequences will not be tolerated. (pp. 88, 89)

Self criticism is the mechanism that makes it possible for us to learn. Readiness to exercise self criticism enables us to expand our perception beyond past positions and to adapt to changing circumstances. Openness to others reflects our readiness to learn and to be always ready to correct our perceptions and expand our mental horizons.

6. Similar and Yet Different

Dialectics of the Leadership Role

Leading role includes but transcends membership in a group or an institution. It is then taken for granted that a leader retains membership, and is perceived as such by the followers. The leader

---

[57] Popper, K. R. (1999). *The Poverty of Historicism.* London: Routledge. (First published 1957.)

shares membership with other members of the group that he is in charge of. Membership is the common umbrella. However, the leader is member in a different capacity. Hence contradiction is built in the role of leader. This contradiction can be formulated as a law in the following statement: *"To be a leader you must be similar enough to be understood, yet different enough to justify your unique position in the group."*

Let us first consider the similarity requirement: First, we have already stated that the first ingredient of similarity is to share membership with the rest of the group. However, the leader's awareness of this as a fact is not enough. The leader must ensure that members continue to feel that the leader's decisions and actions are credible indicators of his continued membership. There are a number of conditions that allow this to happen:

First, the leader must appear to be somewhat familiar, or at least not strange, both in conduct and even in appearance. A minimum degree of similarity allows followers to identify with the leader, or at least, to be able to make sense out of his behavior and conduct as a leader. The path of leadership is blocked if leader and follower are different to the extent they cannot make sense of each other's behavior or communicated messages.

Second, a leader must share, or at least respect, the essential ingredients of the culture of the group — its core values and cherished aspirations.

Third, leader's actions are consistent with the follower's conception of the leadership role in their common culture.

Fourth, naturally, followers do not expect their leader to be a copy of any other member in the group, nor do they expect him to exemplify the *average individual* simply because the average individual does not exist in reality. However, the leader's distinctive characteristics must be somewhat accepted as personal or original, rather than bizarre. In other words, the leader's distinctive features must make sense and are understandable. This places a heavy burden on the leader, namely to assume responsibility for explaining himself or herself. We may call this the burden of managing one's public image.

In short, similarity as explained above allows interpersonal compatibility and facilitates the followers' identification with the leader. Research undertaken by Sherif and Sherif (1953) provides empirical support of this issue:

Almost every study of leadership does reveal superiority (of the leader) over other group members in at least one of many relevant abilities, skills, or traits. But the abilities and skills selected for prominence in the group seem to depend upon the values and ways of the group quite as much as on the personality of the leader ... Thus, as Helen Jennings concluded, the 'why' of leadership appears... not to reside in any personality trait, but in the interpersonal contribution of which the individual becomes capable in a specific setting eliciting such contribution from him.[58] (p. 41)

Why, and in what ways, should the leader be different?

First, the Leader as Integrator

Usually, or preferably, the leader overseas people who are different in character from each other and have different roles to play in the group. So diversity puts a double challenge to the leader, namely to maximize the use of diverse resources, and integrate the efforts of members of the group. Sun Tzu (1983) points out the infinite virtues of diversity that a General must be aware of, and put to good use:

> If a General is ignorant of the principle of adaptability, he must not be entrusted with a position of authority. The skillful employer of men will employ the wise man, the brave man, the covetous man, and the stupid man. For the wise man delights in establishing his merit, the brave man likes to show his courage in action, the covetous man is quick at seizing advantages, and the stupid man has no fear of death. (p. 17)

> There are not more than five musical notes, yet the combinations of these five give rise to more melodies than can ever be heard. There are not more than five primary colors, yet in combination they produce more hues than can ever be seen. There are not more than five cardinal tastes — sour, acid, salt, sweet, bitter — yet combinations of them yield more flavors than can ever be tasted. In battle, however, there are not more than two methods of attack — the direct and the indirect;

---

[58] Verba, S. (1961).

yet these two in combination give rise to an endless series of maneuvers. The direct and the indirect lead to each other in turn. It is like moving in circle — you never exhaust the possibilities of their combination. (pp. 21, 22)

Second, Leader's Position at the Boundary

While being a member of the group, the leader is the only member who is in charge of the group as a whole. He overseas the members' interactions and steers their activities in the service of the group function. But the leader's responsibility extends beyond the group. He has the additional responsibility to regulate the interaction between the group and other groups, whether within the same organization or external to it. I am talking here about a leader of a small unit. But the same principle applies to a CEO whose responsibility is to steer the entire organization in the world at large. To fulfill the boundary role, the leader has to integrate two opposing perspectives, inward and outward. There is ample evidence both from experimental studies of groups and field observations that fulfilling the boundary role enhances the power of the leader in the eyes of the followers. Boundary management confers on the leader what I call, *representational power*. That is when the group leader acts as a representative of his unit *vis-à-vis* the organization. His power is further enhanced if the organization treats him as its representative *vis-à-vis* his own unit. Thus the group leader is then seen to belong both to his group and to the organization. Representational status is lost if the manager is exclusively superior-oriented or subordinate-oriented. The dual perspective and the ability of shifting back and forth between them qualify the leader as integration force. My observations lead me to believe that this feature is very much lacking in most organizations, whether public or private.

Third, Leader as Interpreter

It is the primary responsibility of leaders to interpret the organizational mission to the rank and file. A mission statement is abstract and inert. It comes to life if its relevance to strategies, decisions and actions are demonstrated by those who lead.

Fourth, Leader as Vanguard

I mentioned earlier that the leader must be "similar enough to facilitate followers' identification with him or her". However, identification should not be an end in itself. It is a favorable state of mind that facilitates the leader's assumption of his or her role as a leader. Identification sets the stage for the leader to stand out and realize the uniqueness of his role. Here comes the principle that the leader should be different. The main difference lies in the fact that the group as a whole, and not single individuals, is the leader's burden. The leader has to offer people alternatives to what they want. There comes the time when the leader has to risk making hard decisions that are not popular but necessary for group progress. The leader has to innovate in order to maintain credibility as a leader. Survival of the organization depends on the organization's adaptability to the changes outside. A group or organization propels itself through acts of will, realized by people in leadership position. This means that a leader should attempt to move the group or the organization beyond its current position. In other words, the leader should be an agent of change and continuity. That is, a dual role that calls for careful consideration of surrounding conditions. The leader's influence is enhanced if he demonstrates in action that he is capable of maintaining the group's continuity into the future.

Rationale for Leaders' Autonomy

The will to lead implies the intent to maintain one's autonomy which means the right to be different from the crowd. Conformity as I demonstrated earlier is a form of compliance. Often subordinates may have wrong conceptions of the leader's role, in which case it would be the leader's responsibility to question such conceptions and correct them. In fact autonomy implies more than resistance of conformity to group pressure. It implies resistance to internal pressure of compelling assumptions, biases and idiosyncrasies. Questioning is the means to resist the tyranny of one's thinking. That is the very essence of what we mean by clarity: clarity as a process of questioning, oneself and others.

Autonomy of the leader is required for the creation and survival of the group: A group is inevitably heterogeneous. No human individual can be a copy of another. Even identical twins are dissimilar in a variety of ways. Only an autonomous leader can transcend the differences and create a group spirit. Being different and non-conformist, the leader is free to unify the group, to get members to rally around a mission or identify with a common objective. The autonomous leader can crystallize aspirations and articulate the mood of the group.

Similarity and Differences are Inseparable

I must point out that followers respond to the leader as a whole entity, and not to distinct features of his conduct or character. They do not have in mind two separate lists of similarities and differences. Followers respond to the mix rather than to distinct features. They may later use conscious analysis to explain their overall reaction, whether negative or positive. Often they do not care less about explanations. They simply determine their attitude towards the leader based on "gut feeling". George Herbert Mead (1967)[59] explains how uniqueness of great leaders is a function of the dialectics of similarity and difference. He uses the term "genius" to denote a leader who succeeds to create a social movement:

> The behavior of a genius is socially conditioned just as that of an ordinary individual is; and his achievements are the results of, or are responses to, social stimuli just as those of an ordinary individual are. The genius, like the ordinary individual comes back at himself from the standpoint of the organized social group to which he belongs and the attitudes of that group toward any project in which he becomes involved; and he responds to this generalized attitude of the group with a definite attitude of his own toward the given project just as the ordinary individual does. But this definite attitude of his own with which he responds to the generalized attitude of the group is unique and original in the case of the genius,

---

[59] Mead, G. H. (1962). *Mind, Self, and Society from the Standpoint of a Social Behaviorist.* Chicago: The University of Chicago Press (first published 1934).

whereas it is not so in the case of the ordinary individual; and it is this uniqueness and originality of his response to a given social situation or problem or project — which nevertheless conditions his behavior no less than it does that of the ordinary individual — that distinguishes the genius from the ordinary individual. (p. 216)

7. Energy

Leadership as Flow of Energy

Since personality is a bio-psycho-social system, it was natural that I include the topic of energy in building up my model of leadership. I do not see how we can ignore the fact that the human person, leader or not is endowed with a body, the source of energy, the life source without which no action would be possible. To understand a leader's conduct, we must consider the following related variables: availability of energy rather than consummated energy, direction of energy, and outcome of energy expenditure.

Leadership may well be defined as the flow of energy from a human person (a leader) to another (a follower). In fact the word "influence" encapsulates this very fact. It is derived from the Latin verb *fluere*, meaning to flow into. There has been much talk about the dynamism of a leader with the view that exertion of energy is a necessary requirement for effective leadership. There is less consideration for deliberate management of available energy or economic use of energy. This bias is associated with the American model of leadership that emphasizes dominance, aggressiveness and assertiveness, or the dynamic impact of the leader on other people and the world at large. In such dynamic notions, there seems to be less concern for regulation of one's energy, economy of energy, direction of energy, or impact of the dynamic leader on energies of people he or she leads. It is true that a leader may be a source of energy but he may also drain the energy out of people. Leaders, especially those endowed with charisma can arouse the enthusiasm of the followers. Enthusiasm can be infectious but it can ultimately have a draining effect. An overactive leader may waste his own energy and may do the same to energy resources of his or her group.

Energy Management

Managers need to be reminded that there is a world of difference between *kinetic energy* and *potential energy*. Kinetic (Greek *kinētikos*) means pertaining to, or producing motion. Kinetic energy is energy in action, or energy engaged in motion, but "potential energy" is energy at rest, or not manifested in actual work. In other words, kinetic energy is energy in the process of being expended while potential energy is the stored energy, or technically speaking, the available energy.

The issue therefore is not for dynamism in absolute terms but the wise deployment of energy. Our concern should therefore be for availability of energy at all times. Of equal importance is the leader's awareness of the impact of his own energy on the recipients of his or her influence. Typically, managers tend to stress manifest exertion of energy rather than wise deployment of energy resources, their own and their charges. *The index of vitality of a system lies not in how much energy the system expends but how much energy is kept in store.*

Interestingly experienced leaders seem to heed this principle in their work habits as well as in their leadership behavior. Take, for example, Field Marshall Montgomery. Montgomery's actual conduct in the midst of war has been diametrically opposed to exertion of energy. Lewin writes in his biography of Montgomery:

> Montgomery used to take dinner and then retire to bed with strict instructions that he must not be disturbed except in a crisis. R. W. Thompson once coined a phrase which in this context is most apt. Montgomery, he writes, "had the knack of creating oases of serenity around himself." There are many witnesses to this charismatic gift. When, for example, Goronwy Rees, a brilliant Fellow of All Souls, Oxford, was posted to Montgomery's staff in those later days when he was in charge of South-Eastern Command, Rees approached his first interview with a natural trepidation. But he later remembered "that air of calm and peace which he carried with him was so strong that after a moment my panic and alarm began to die away; it was something which one felt to be almost incongruous in a soldier." At a higher level, I recall how Sir Miles Dempsey told me that, when he was commanding Second Army in Normandy, he never failed, at bad moments, to be reinvigorated by a visit to Montgomery, and that the

Field Marshal, with his cheerful smile and his confident air, had a way of turning apparent difficulties into phantoms. The habit of undisturbed night and the daily routine were, in fact, no more than particular aspects of something which by now was deeply rooted in Montgomery's nature. He was sure of himself. (p. 29)

The author cites an illustrative incident:

It must have been during the night of 14 or 15 May that a staff officer, obviously unaware of the sanctity of Montgomery's couch, roused him to report that the Germans had entered Louvain. Montgomery true to form replied, "Go away and don't bother me. Tell the brigadier in Louvain to turn them out" which was done.

The same living philosophy has long been known in Eastern annals. *The Tao of Tai-Chi* stresses the intimate connection between *effortlessness* and effective action:

... the mind during practice should be like a hawk slowly circling high up in effortless flight, but falling like a stone upon the rabbit it spies far below. Stillness is concealed within the constant flying action. The development of bodily relaxation with strong mental intention after constant practice illustrates how Tai-Chi may return to Wu-Chi. Action is to be hidden behind apparent stillness, just as a cat, waiting motionless in front of a mouse hole is poised for a deadly pounce the instant the mouse appears. Thus one should be concentrated at all times without using outer force. Finally, although the movements are large and stretched at first, they become more subtle during the more advanced stages. The emphasis shifts from the outside form to the inside one. During the final stage no outward movement can be detected; yet a master, when touched can throw one across the room. (pp. 107, 108)

Centuries before modern scientists discover the properties of energy Sun Tzu knew the difference between kinetic and potential energy and utilized the knowledge in war. In the *Art of War* he pointed out that: "energy may be likened to the bending of crossbow, decision, to the releasing of the trigger." The simile implies that the force which the general needs is the potential energy that is stored up in the bent crossbow until released by the finger at the proper time.[60] Sun Tzu applied his conception of energy to what he called the "Stratagem of using the sheathed sword":

> The skillful leader subdues the enemy's troops without any fighting; he captures their cities without laying siege to them; he overthrows their kingdom without lengthy operations in the field. With his forces intact he disputes the mastery of the empire, and thus, without losing a man, his triumph is complete. (p. 16)

Bertrand Russell pointed out the danger inherent in enthusiasm:

> Revivalist enthusiasm, such as that of the Nazis, rouses admiration in many through the energy and apparent self-abnegation that it generates. Collective excitement, involving indifference to pain and even to death, is historically not uncommon. Where it exists, liberty is impossible. The enthusiasts can only be restrained by force, and if they are not restrained they will use force against others. I remember a Bolshevik whom I met in Peking in 1920, who marched up and down, the room exclaiming with complete truth: "If we do not keel zem, zey vill keel us!" The existence of this mood on one side of course generates the same mood on the other side; the consequence is a fight to a finish, in which everything is subordinated to victory. During the fight, the government acquires despotic power for military reasons; at the end, if victorious, it uses its power first to crush what remains of the enemy, and then to secure the continuance of its dictatorship over its own supporters. The result is something quite different from what was fought for by the enthusiasts. Enthusiasm, while it can achieve certain results, can hardly ever achieve those that it desires. To admire collective enthusiasm is reckless and irresponsible, for its fruits are fierceness, war, death, and slavery. (p. 201)

---

[60] Sun Tzu (1983), p. 22.

Pure Dynamism

It is easy to detect pathology when a person's energy diminishes to the level of lethargy, apathy or indifference. But it is much more difficult to detect pathology in manifestations at the excessive level of expenditure of energy. We tend to be biased in favor of any form of enthusiasm or dynamism. This brings to mind the insightful concept of *pure dynamism* that Albert Camus (1951) discussed in his book *L'homme révolté* (or the rebel). Camus focused on the condition of an overactive person who is constantly on the go: "Men of action in the absence of faith are left with nothing to believe in other than action." What Camus meant by "pure dynamism" is the primitive type of striving or perpetual action orientation at the level of naked force, the force that springs directly from the biological depths of the human person. He uses this concept in describing Hitler's revolution. According to Camus pure dynamism explains the tragedy in Germany under the Nazis:

> Germany, shaken from the roots by a war without precedence, defeated, and economically ruined, had no more values to hold on to ... epidemic of suicide that plagued the entire country between the two wars exposed the nation's state of mental confusion. Those in the grip of utter despair could not restore faith through reasoning. Only through passion could they regain it, and that was the passion that springs from despair: humiliation and hatred. ... Thus, in the absence of the morality of Goethe, 1933 Germany opted for, and surrendered to the decadent morals of the gang ... The morals of the gang being an exhaustible supply of triumph and vengeance, defeat and resentment. (p. 223, my translation)

The notion of "pure dynamism" recurs in accounts given at Nuremburg by Nazi characters. Frank, for example, pointed out that "hatred of form" animated Hitler. Camus comments:

> It is true that this man [Hitler] was but a force in perpetual movement, directed and rendered more efficacious by shrewd calculations and inexorable tactical clairvoyance. Even his physical build, mediocre and commonplace as it has been, was not a hindrance: it endeared him to the masses. *Action alone kept him on his feet. To be is to act.*

> That explains why Hitler and his regime could not do
> without enemies. Fanatical dandies as they were, they could
> not define themselves except relative to their enemies.
> (p. 224)

During Nuremburg trials, Rosenberg likened life to a marching column constantly on the go, "it is the style of the marching what matters, the destination or where the march is heading is of less importance". Rosenberg's pompous comment, says Camus, lays open the biological foundations of Hitler's entire foreign policy. He adds that Hitler was "history in its purest form". To Hitler, *becoming* was more worthy than just living. Hitler preached intimate identification with the stream of life. But it is life at the lowest level that challenges any superior reality.

I am aware of course that pure dynamism as described by Camus is an extreme phenomenon realized by a minority of leaders. But such minority does exist in reality and their dynamism has devastating effects on masses of people. They do exist not only at a high level of the power structures, but also at the lower level. And not only in governing but also, which is equally dangerous, in education. Prevalent leadership models seem biased in favor of action orientation, dominance, competitiveness. Maybe we ought to counter this bias by more investment in the virtues of reflection, impulse control, cooperativeness, and serenity. Alternative sources of power are more diverse than we think. But let us go back to the prerequisites.

Interdependence and Value of the Prerequisites

If you ask people to indicate the characteristics of effective leaders, you are going to get long lists of characteristics covering a wide spectrum of personality sphere. They will agree on some characteristics and differ on others. But the list you compile from different people will not allow us to grasp the essential features that apply to all types of leaders. Furthermore, different characteristics have different weights. The value of the proposed prerequisites is this: they guide us in a systematic way to the various requirements that people usually list. For example the "will to lead" applies to any leader irrespective of the style he or she adopts. It draws our attention to the motivational basis of leadership efforts, the strength of intention to lead. The will to lead refers to the motivational force and this force has to be guided by cognition. That is where clarity comes into the picture to guide the leader's choices: distinguish between what is essential and what is peripheral or irrelevant, between what is urgent and what is less urgent and so on. In short, prerequisites operate in concert to produce coherent and stable patterns of behavior. They should serve as regulatory principles.

The reader may wonder why I listed only five prerequisites. My answer is that I started out with two, the "will to lead" and "clarity". Both variables emerged spontaneously from first-hand observation, self reports and biographical accounts of leaders. Initial observations were complemented by simple questionnaires. The questionnaires yielded rich information in a more formal way. The rest of the prerequisites forced themselves on my mind in the course of interviews or from responses to a variety of surveys. The reader may consult the appendices to identify the prerequisites in many of the responses given spontaneously by respondents to surveys that I conducted. The last prerequisite to hit me with a bang was energy. And yet going over the responses to various questionnaires, I found out that the energy has been there all the time. Why did I miss that enormous number of responses referring to energy? Obviously I was shying away from any response that spells biology. Once I was confronted with this bias, I began to see clearly the role energy plays in determining the way a manager goes about his daily tasks — his or her style if you wish; and the impact of the manager's energy output on his or her subordinates.

The Cultural Dilemma

Prerequisites helped me resolve a chronic dilemma: I lived, taught and ran seminars in different countries around the globe. I also used psychological instruments designed in the US or UK. Tests measuring aspects of leadership convinced me that there are several models of leadership that are at variance with Western models, especially with regard to deciding the criteria of leadership effectiveness. I had no scientific evidence to confirm or deny the applicability of such models to non-Western cultures, but I had glaring observations against such applicability. I had the opportunity of testing few successful leaders in Asian countries who, to my surprise, obtained low scores on Western indicators of leadership or traits related to leadership such as dominance or competitiveness. Occasionally I would come across leaders who manifest Western patterns in their leadership style. I had no way of telling whether their style has been a function of acculturation while studying and working in the US.

Thus I decided to focus on prerequisites and leave the issue of specific traits to be decided by people belonging to any culture. Analogies from biology may better illustrate what is meant by prerequisites *vis-à-vis* actual traits or functions. Physical health and biochemical balance requires sufficient amounts of vitamins and minerals. All are essential. However, some have more weight than others. For example, zinc is called the "growth" mineral. It is essential at every stage of life for growth and development. Although zinc is a trace mineral like many other trace minerals, it carries more weight than its trace designation implies. Zinc is a critical part of nucleic acid — the basic ingredient in the development of every single human cell. In all, zinc works with at least 70 different enzymes that perform a wide variety of essential functions throughout the body. Without zinc, these enzymes may not perform properly. Zinc is also necessary to form tissues, such as skin, organs and bones. Zinc promotes sensation and appetite. So, just as zinc is needed to activate at least 70 different enzymes, each of the proposed prerequisites triggers many other personality dynamics. Take, for example, the will to lead. You can be very dominant but prefer to compete in business contests, or in Olympic Games, or in chess games, or in dramatics.

I presented prerequisites here separately and in an arbitrary sequence one after the other. This may give the impression that they are separate in reality which they are not. On paper we can afford to conceptualize for the sake of clarity. But in life what we observe is a person in the act of leading. It is the act that matters. The thing that comes out clearly is that the prerequisites dovetail, interact and even interpenetrate. When you ask a person about how his boss communicates, inevitably he or she will refer to the boss's enthusiasm or lethargy, namely the amount of energy the boss injects into his message. He may also refer to the fact that the boss, being enthusiastic, overloads you with information leaving you without clarity about the central issues in the message. Each concept connected my mind to earlier concepts that seemed unrelated before. For instance, energy brought to mind what I had learnt about the second law of thermodynamics, namely the law of entropy. This law drew my attention to the difference between potential and kinetic energy and the vital importance of conserving energy in conducting one's affairs. Conserving energy connected me to the wisdom inherent in Eastern philosophies and explained Bertrand Russell's emphasis on the function of leisure in an article entitled "in praise of idleness".

It is as if each concept has intrinsic magnetic force that pulls out of the mind other concepts. That is what scientists call the "heuristic" value of a theory, namely the power of the theory to raise questions or suggest fresh hypotheses leading to new avenues of inquiry. And now that we have the concepts in mind, we can see more clearly into the behavior we call leading or following. In other words, we can make more sense of the leaders' and followers' actions. How else could I have interpreted influence as flow of energy between leaders and followers? I could also explain theories of leadership in terms of the direction of energy implicit in the theory. For example, the intrapersonal approach to leadership derives from the assumption that a leader is a *cause* of events. In other words, energy flows from the leader to the followers when in fact influence is reciprocal. Reciprocity implies that energy flows back and forth between leaders and followers and among followers as well and in relation to the energy engendered by the leader's interventions.

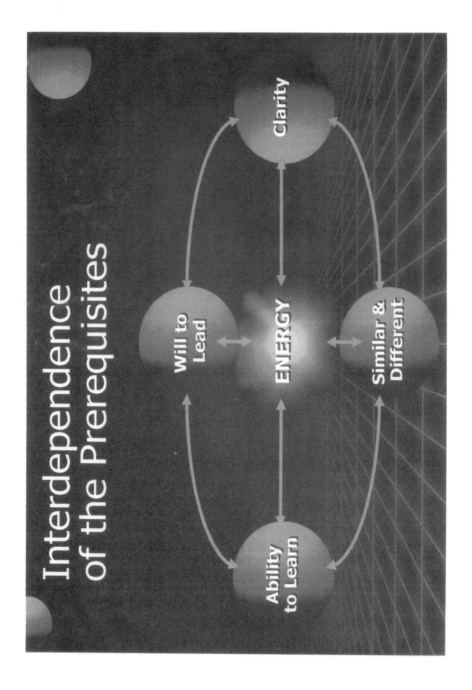

Crisis of Leadership

Having dealt with managers around the world for more than three decades, I am struck by the omnipresence of disappointment with leadership. Young people going into management or into politics harbor a great deal of skepticism or, what is worse, cynicism. A growing lexicon of new terms reflects discontent in various countries: terms such as *cleptocracy*, plutocracy, corruption, nepotism, greed, exploitation, subservience to foreign powers, and more, point to serious problems. Nowadays, we can easily find in high places tyrants, mass murderers, psychopaths, sexual deviants, former drug abusers, and recovered or non-recovered alcoholics. Furthermore, we know of leaders who ascended to power by deceit, connivance and opportunism. Often they become captive of mafia-like coalitions of powerful individuals. Such "leaders" remain too long in their positions thanks either to external support or passive compliance of their people or a combination of both. They rule but do not lead. Often they mislead.

We are witnessing complete failure of moral leadership at the highest levels. This is taking place even in a country that invented management science, offers the finest leadership programs, and houses reputable schools of business and public administration. Jeffrey Toobin wrote in *The New Yorker Magazine*[61]:

---

[61] Issue of 22 March 2004.

The cult of the chief executive reached its apogee in the nineteen-nineties, a period when CEOs seemed not so much to serve their companies as to embody them. Certainly, there was a Time Warner independent of Gerald Levin, and Disney and General Electric existed beyond Michael Eisner and Jack Welch. Yet these executives, and others like them, were compensated as if they single-handedly controlled the fates of their companies. In the late eighties, a seven-figure salary was a lot to pay a CEO; by the late nineties, nine-figure fortunes were routine. The chairman of General Motors, for example, made five hundred and seventy-five thousand dollars in base salary in 1991 and just over two million in 2000. Michael Ovitz, at Disney, got a severance package worth somewhere between ninety and a hundred and thirty million dollars. But how much difference did most of these executives make? They took credit when the nation's economy made almost every business leader look good, and they blamed the fates when times turned hard. Many were, in essence, lavishly paid bureaucrats — caretakers more than creators.

Policy of meritocracy in selection of leaders failed to curb corruption in France, Germany, England or Japan.

Success as Index of Effectiveness

There are, of course, worthy leaders who arrived at their positions thanks to exceptional talents and past record of achievements. Usually, however, success of such leaders is explained in terms of their unique qualities while ignoring the help they got from many of their associates and subordinates. The intrapersonal bias is endemic. Meanwhile many worthy leaders fail to achieve the goals they set out to achieve for no fault of their own. I can site several examples from my own observations of many government leaders that were chucked out of their jobs despite their eminence and record of achievements. The reason, I am sorry to say, was that their successes had caught the public eye, something a despotic ruler could not tolerate.

We need to spell out in no ambiguous terms criteria for what we consider *success* in leading, or *outcomes* of leading performance. Furthermore, we also need to differentiate clearly between success in rising to a high position and the ability of the power holders to utilize power in the service of their people.

A related subject is what constitutes ideal leadership. What type is the best for leadership position? "This is always the wrong question," says Mary McCaulley. Looking at samples of people who took the Meyers Briggs Type Indicator test (MBTI) McCaulley found that all sixteen types identified by the MBTI "end up in every position, doing every type of work, playing every role." She also found "that most positions, and work, and roles, have characteristic type distribution, with some types less frequent." McCaulley concludes:

> In all the research samples of substantial size, all or virtually all types were represented among the leaders. There is no type that is doomed to "follower", nor obviously, is every person in a particular type necessarily going to be a leader. A lot will depend on how leadership is defined. (pp. 22, 23)

Leader's Cognitive Functions

Much of the literature stresses the cognitive functions of leaders within which intelligence occupies a dominant position. There are strong reasons calling for a revision of this bias:

First, correlations between leader intelligence and leader performance have been consistently low, as shown by Fiedler (1970 & 1993) and other researchers.

Second, intelligence as defined by IQ tests is an estimate of probability or potentiality. Unfortunately, one can be endowed by high potential and yet makes poor decisions which a person with mediocre intelligence does not make. Let us not forget that the mistakes that an intelligent person commits tend to be far more serious than the mistakes committed by a mentally retarded. And if that intelligent person happened to hold a leadership position, the mistakes he commits can have devastating effect on masses of people.

Third, IQ tests are useful tools in the assessment of academic types of cognitive functions but fail to predict creativity. I am not arguing against the value of intelligence tests. I have made a living out of using them. Rather, I am stressing their limitations that no responsible psychologist ignores, particularly when the issue is to predict creativity. Promising attempts have been made to fill in this gap. Naturally a combination of the usual IQ tests and measures of creativity enhance our selection procedures. Furthermore, great feats of creative accomplishments require a minimum level of intelligence as measured by existing IQ tests. The emergence of valid tests of creativity would not by any means discredit the value of the current IQ tests.

Fourth, evidence is steadily growing in favor of a third type of intelligence, namely practical intelligence. Practical intelligence seems quite different from the intelligence that is measured by IQ tests. Practical intelligence may be roughly defined as competence in everyday living. The work by Sternberg and Wagner (1986) deserves our attention.[62]

Fifth, much of the work on cognitive functioning depends on single-culture models. Many research programs demonstrate the potential hazards of single-culture research. For example, Greenfield (1997) found that it means a different thing to take a test among Mayan children than it does among most children in the United States. Mayan expectation is that collaboration is permissible and that it is rather unnatural *not* to collaborate. The work of Markus and Kitayama (1991), suggest different "cultural constructions" of the self in individualistic as opposed to collectivistic cultures. Nisbett (2003) has found that some cultures, especially Asian ones, tend to be more dialectical in their thinking, whereas other cultures, such as European and North American cultures tend to be more linear. What appear to be differences in general intelligence may in fact be differences in cultural properties (Helms-Lorenz, Van de Vijver, & Poortinga, 2003).

I had long and intimate experience in Egypt using intelligence tests designed in the US and adapted to the Arabic language. My Egyptian subjects tended to obtain much lower scores on the performance parts of the tests than on the verbal parts. Similar results in the US would have serious implications. For example, it would at least raise the issue of brain damage. Careful enquiry provided simple and direct explanation for this phenomenon. Performance tests designed in the US require the use of delicate materials such as colored blocks, small polished cards, and caricature drawings. To the average Egyptian adults — and even to many Egyptian children — such materials

---

[62] Sternberg, R. J. (2004). Culture and Intelligence. *American Psychologist*, Vol. 99, No. 5, pp. 325–338.

looked like silly toys that they rarely use. They were more accustomed to handling clubs, bricks, branches of trees and the like. They wade in canals for fishing, climb trees and ride donkeys. Cultural meanings of objects used in tests should be taken into consideration.

Sternberg (2004) identifies several flaws in single-culture studies: they introduce limited definitions of psychological phenomena and problems; engender risks of unwarranted assumptions about the phenomena under investigation; raise questions about the *cultural generalizability* of findings; and represent lost opportunities to collaborate and develop psychology around the world.

In our enthusiasm for scientific thinking and formal logic we may ignore common sense. We ought to ponder Wittgenstein's message, "Do not think, just look" as reminder of the power of observation, simplicity, and use of common language. Bergson, the French philosopher and one of the great minds of the twentieth century, considers intellect to be "unduly passive and merely contemplative." In contrast, intuition is able "to perform miracles". Bergson reminds us that "all evolution is due to desire and there is no limit to what can be achieved if desire is sufficiently passionate". Systematized rational thinking narrows one's perspective and produces rigidities in place of creative openness to discovery and knowledge.

We often talk about a visionary leader and a leader that is not visionary. Any human being irrespective of the level of intelligence can have a vision or be aroused by a vision. After all, imagination precedes logical thinking in mental development. Imagination is more primitive and more powerful than rational reasoning. But the journey from a vision to its realization is a long and arduous one. Its realization requires transformation to suit the changing circumstances and the help of many people who are moved by its plausibility.

In conclusion, to be on the right track in the assessment of leaders' effectiveness we need to expand our conception of cognition to include non-intellective components. Furthermore, cognition must be placed within the context of personality as a whole. Emotive factors must be considered. We need not revert to semi-scientific terms such as "lateral thinking" or "emotional IQ". Our common language already includes the terms we need — wisdom and good judgment are global enough to integrate all the vital factors, cognitive and otherwise that Bergson alluded to. Furthermore wisdom and good judgment presuppose the moral dimension in the absence of which leading degenerates into misleading.

Failure of Social Science

Social sciences, their advancement notwithstanding, have not been able to provide solutions to major problems of the human kind. Crime is on the increase and prison system has failed to correct, rehabilitate or even to deter. Revolving door phenomenon characterizes both prisons and mental hospitals. Wars and social upheavals are raging everywhere. Economic globalization has been matched by globalization of terrorism. Corruption in high places is endemic.

Many factors contribute to the failure of social sciences in improving the human condition. One is excessive specialization. Specialists whether in psychology, anthropology or economics are trained to become experts in a very constricted domain. In fact universities rarely provide encouragement for generalists. Now respectability is associated with depth of specialization. No doubt we need specialists but failing a movement of integration, there is no way that any specialized expertise can solve any of the human problems. Human problems are both complex and complicated, requiring solutions engendered by integrated view or interdisciplinary perspective. Excessive specialization characterizes the field of psychology, one of the cornerstones of the fields of organization management.

Whitehead's Diagnosis[63]

As early as 1925 Alfred Whitehead, the great philosopher mathematician warned us against the dangers of narrow specialization. He pointed out that a major problem confronting the modern world is "the discovery of the method of training professionals, who specialize in particular regions of thought and thereby progressively add to the sum of knowledge within their respective limitations of subject." Whitehead has this to say about the dangers of this phenomenon:

---

[63] Whitehead, Alfred North (1953). *Science and the Modern World*. New York: The Free Press (first published 1925).

This situation has its dangers. It produces minds in a groove. Each profession makes progress, but it is progress in its own groove. Now to be mentally in a groove is to live in contemplating a given set of abstractions. The groove prevents straying across country, and the abstraction abstracts from something to which no further attention is paid. *But there is no groove of abstractions which is adequate for the comprehension of human life.* Thus in the modern world, the celibacy of the medieval learned class has been replaced by a celibacy of the intellect which is divorced from the concrete contemplation of the complete facts. Of course, no one is merely a mathematician, or merely a lawyer. People have lives outside their professions or their businesses. But the point is the restraint of serious thought within a groove. The remainder of life is treated superficially, with the imperfect categories of thought derived from one profession. (pp. 196, 197)

Whitehead goes on to stress the widespread dangers of this phenomenon:

This criticism of modern life applies throughout in whatever sense you construe the meaning of a community. It holds if you apply it to a nation, a city, a district, an institution, a family, or even to an individual. There is a development of particular abstractions, and a contraction of concrete appreciation. The whole is lost in one of its aspects. It is not necessary for my point that I should maintain that our directive wisdom, either as individuals or as communities, is less now than in the past. Perhaps it has slightly improved. But the novel pace of progress requires a greater force of direction if disasters are to be avoided. The point is that the discoveries of the nineteenth century were in the direction of professionalism, so that we are left with no expansion of wisdom and with greater need of it.

Whitehead concludes that without wisdom, we cannot solve the problems of the modern world. But to him, wisdom is a complex and dynamic construct that develops in time:

Wisdom is the fruit of a balanced development. It is this balanced growth of individuality which it should be the aim of education to secure. The most useful discoveries for the immediate future would concern the furtherance of this aim without detriment to the necessary intellectual professionalism. ... (pp. 197, 198)

Specialization seems to have infected the field of humanities. Edward Said (1983)[64] lamented this phenomenon:

> For the relatively unmarketable humanists whose wares are "soft" and whose expertise is almost by definition marginal, their constituency is a fixed one composed of other humanist students, government and corporate executives and media employees, who use the humanist to assure a harmless place for "the humanities" or culture or literature in the society. I hasten to recall, however, that this is the role voluntarily accepted by humanists whose notion of what they do is neutralized, specialized and nonpolitical in the extreme. To an alarming degree, the present continuation of the humanities depends, I think, on the sustained self-purification of humanists, for whom the ethic of specialization has become equivalent to minimizing the content of their work and increasing the composite wall of guild consciousness, social authority and exclusionary discipline around themselves. Opponents are therefore not people in disagreement with the constituency but people to be kept out, non-experts and non-specialists, for the most part. (p. 152)

Specialization translates confinement and enclosure, leading ultimately to alienation from the masses. Jargon replaces common language of the street, and abstractions replace common sense. Theories fail do provide understanding of reality. Expert power inflates and before we know it we have a burgeoning special interest group in competition with other interest groups. A case of point is the conflict between clinical psychologists and psychiatrists, or the nursing profession versus the medical profession, or the chiropractic against the medical profession, and so on *ad infinitum*.

---

[64] Said, E. (1983). Opponents, Audiences, Constituencies and Community. In H. Foster (editor). *The Anti-Aesthetic: Essays on Postmodern Culture*. New York: The New Press, pp. 135–159.

Psychologism

Mills C. Wright (1967)[65] decries the same phenomenon in the field of psychology:

> "Psychologism" refers to the attempt to explain social phenomena in terms of facts and theories about the make-up of individuals. Historically, as a doctrine, it rests upon an explicit metaphysical denial of the reality of social structure. At other times, its adherents may set forth a conception of structure which reduces it, so far as explanations are concerned, to a set of milieux. In a still more general way, and of more direct interest to our concern with the current research policies of social science, psychologism rests upon the idea that if we study a series of individuals and their milieu, the results of our studies in some way can be added up to a knowledge of social structure. (p. 47)

Specialization in the scientific field has its advantages, no doubt. My critique is not directed at specialization as such but focused on the attempts to solve human problems by techniques derived from the perspective of a single discipline. Such attempts are futile because human problems are usually over-determined, namely they are product of the convergence of several forces, an intricate process that takes place in a specified historical time.

Spawning Technology

What we must guard against is the spawning of technology from early scientific discoveries before we are sure about its validity or its implications to the human condition. Technology must be adequately assimilated before any attempt to derive policy from it. What is worse than specialization in a scientific discipline is specialization in the use of a technique without adequate training in the scientific background of the technique. This is becoming a very serious problem in the field of management development. Individuals who have no background in psychology can easily get certification in the use of a

---

[65] Mills C. Wright (1967). *The Sociological Imagination*. London: Oxford University Press.

single psychological instrument. The professional psychologist does not interpret the test results directly but via his or her knowledge and long experience related to the psychology of the human person as a whole. Typically, the lay practitioner takes one step further — he / she proceeds from the findings of a single instrument to provide counseling. Naturally the practitioner draws on his own lay experience to complement the test results which by itself cannot generate adequate policy for living. The danger does not come from counseling as such but from claiming that counseling comes directly and exclusively from a scientifically-based instrument. I have no quarrel with counseling based on the wisdom of a lay counselor. After all, any person with experience and integrity can provide valuable counsel to a less experienced client in need of emotional support.

Leadership is no more a natural phenomenon to be observed where it takes place in society. It became what we study in management development programs or institutions of public administration. Thus psychology has been sucked into consumerism. Leadership should be studied in the wider political and social context. Leadership involves all of us. It can retain our dignity as human persons but it can also debase and dehumanize us. People should define leadership for themselves since they have a stake in it.

The field of leadership suffers from a congestion and informational overload. Difficult problems of terminology, method, and theoretical formulations beset it from all sides. The pressing need is not for more facts or more data: rather, it is for conceptual schemes and systematic theories into which we may fit the facts we have and the facts we shall gather in the future. Also needed are more precise and explicit techniques of data gathering so that the reliability and validity of data we accumulate can be estimated.

Another deplorable feature in modern times is the almost religious faith in technology. This faith has disastrous consequences in the political sphere. A case in point is the sense of omnipotence of a great power that relied totally on advanced technology in its attempt to conquer a less advanced sovereign nation. Here we witness the imbalance in human development, namely the fact that physical sciences is far ahead of the state of development in human sciences.

Then there is the tendency to exclude morality whether in research or in application of techniques in policy making. I do not see how we can avoid the moral implications of theories or practices in matters that affect human relations and the very existence of social groups. In fact what we call now "social", or "human sciences" used to be called "moral sciences", the word "moral" was considered equivalent to "human".

Final Statement

I would not end this book without stressing the moral dimension in leadership. I am struck by a universal phenomenon, namely, a wave of designing mission statements in most organizations. The curious thing is that many of these organizations have been in existence for decades. I wonder why all of a sudden the management of such organizations felt constrained to justify their existence through written statements. There is nothing wrong with that if the reason for spelling out a mission at this late hour were to clarify perceived ambiguity of the organization's purpose for existence or to spell out change in its direction. What struck me in particular is that each statement I had the chance to go over is followed by, or includes reference to integrity. It is as if integrity were not taken for granted. Could that be due to the fact that corruption and abuse of authority have become endemic in modern corporations and that integrity has to be stressed in a formal way? I believe that organizations need only be consistent in enforcing rules, regulations and strict code of ethics. The word "organization" itself implies the upholding of social order. Furthermore the word "leading" presupposes moral integrity — after all, *leading is leading not misleading*.

Bibliography

Allport, G. (1968). *The Person in Psychology: Selected Essays*. Boston: Beacon Press.

Anger, N. (1990, July 17). Parasites take the biological spotlight. *The New York Times*.

Arrow, K. J. (1974*)*. *The Limits of Organization*. New York: W. W. Norton.

Badaracco, Jr., J. L. & Ellsworth, R. R. (1989). *Leadership and the Quest for Integrity*. Boston, Mass.: Harvard Business School.

Barrett, W. (1979). *The Illusion of Technique*. Long Island, NY: Anchor Press.

Becker, E. (1971). *The Lost Science of Man*. New York: George Braziller.

Belasco, J. A. & Stayer, R. C. (1993). *Flight of the Buffalo: Soaring, Learning to Let Employees Lead*. New York: Warner Books.

Bennis, W. and Nanus, B. (1985). *Leaders: The Strategies for Taking Charge*. New York: Harper & Row.

Berne, E. (1966). *The Structure and Dynamics of Organizations and Groups*. New York: Grove Press.

Borger, R. & Cioffi, F. (eds.) (1978). *Explanations in the Behavioral Sciences*. Cambridge, UK: Cambridge University Press.

Bergson, H. (1998). *Creative Evolution*. (Transl. A. Michell.) Mineola, NY: Dover Publications.

Camus, A. (1951). *L'homme revolté*. Paris: Gallimard.

Carlyle, T. (1966). *On Heroes, Hero Worship and the Heroic in History*. University of Nebraska Press. (First published as lectures in 1841.)

Carril, P. (1997). *The Smart Takes from the Strong*. New York: Simon & Schuster.

Chandler, D. G. (1988). *The Military Maxims of Napoleon*. (Trans. G. C. D. Aguilar.) New York: Macmillan.

Chemers, M. M. & Ayman, R. (eds.) (1992). *Leadership Theory and Research: Perspectives and Directions*. San Diego, CA: Academic Press.

Cottingham, J. (ed.) (1999). *The Cambridge Companion to Descartes*. Cambridge, UK: Cambridge University Press.

Crane, D. B. & Eccles, R. G. (1978, November–December). Commercial Banks: Taking Shape for Turbulent Times. *Harvard Business Review*, pp. 94–100.

De La Boétie, É. (1983). *Discours de la servitude volontaire*. [A treatise on voluntary slavery.] Paris: Flammarion. (First published 1574.)

Devito, J. A. (1986). *The Communication Handbook: A Dictionary*. New York: Harper & Row.

Dynes, R. R. & Quarantelli, E. L. (1972). *A Perspective on Disaster Planning*. Washington, DC: Defense Civil Preparedness Agency, Department of Defense.

El-Meligi, A. M. & Surkis, J. (1977). The Scientific Study of Inner Experience: A General Systems Approach. *Orthomolecular Psychiatry*, VI (3), 219–230.

Feldman, D. C. (1967). A contingency theory of socialization. *Administrative Science Quarterly*, *21*, 433–452.

Feldman, D. C. (1988). *Managing Careers in Organizations.* Glenview, IL: Scott, Foresman.

Fiedler, F. E. (1993). The leadership situation and the black box in contingency theory. In M. M. Chemers & R. Ayman (eds.) *Leadership Theory and Research: Perspectives and Directions.* San Diego, CA: Academic Press, pp. 1–28.

Flew, A. (1985). *Thinking about Social Thinking: The Philosophy of Social Sciences.* New York: Basil Blackwell.

Foster, H. (ed.) (1983). *The Anti-Aesthetic: Essays on Postmodern Culture.* New York: The New Press.

Hall, E. T. (1977). *Beyond Culture.* Garden City, New York: Anchor Books / Doubleday.

Heintz, P. (1973). *The Future of Development.* Bern: Hans Huber.

Heller, T. & Van Til, J. (1982). Leadership and followership: Some summary propositions. *Journal of Applied Behavioral Science*, **18(3)**, pp. 405–414.

Hirschhorn, L. & Gilmore, T. (1992, May–June). The new boundaries of the "boundaryless" organization. *Harvard Business Review*, 104115. [Reprint 92304.]

Hoch, P. H. & Zubin, J. (1958). *Psychopathology of Communication.* New York: Grune & Stratton.

Horton, D. & Wohl, R. R. (1976). Mass communication and parasocial interaction. In J. E. Combs & M. W. Mansfield (eds.) *Drama in Life: The Uses of Communication in Society.* New York: Hastings House, pp. 212–227.

Ibn Khaldun (1981). *The Muqaddemah: An Introduction to History.* (Transl. F. Rosenthal.) Princeton, NJ: Princeton University Press. (Original work published in 1377.)

James, W. (1947). *Selected Papers on Philosophy.* New York: E. P. Dutton. (First published 1917.)

Janis, I. (1972). *Victims of Groupthink: A Psychological Study of Foreign Policy Decisions and Fiascos.* Boston: Houghton Mifflin.

Jacques, E. (1990, January–February). In praise of hierarchy. *Harvard Business Review*, pp. 127–133.

Jones, G. R. (1986). Socialization tactics, self-efficacy, and newcomers' adjustments to organizations. *Academy of Management Journal, 29*, pp. 262–279.

Korzybski, A. (1973). *Science and Sanity: An Introduction to Non-Aristotelian Systems and General Semantics.* Lakeville, Connecticut: The International Non-Aristotelian Company (Fourth Edition).

Lasswell, H. D. (1977). *Psychopathology and Politics.* Chicago: The University of Chicago Press. (First published 1930.)

Lewin, R. (1971). *Montgomery: A Military Commander.* New York: Stein & Day.

Lorenz, K. (1979). *Man Meets Dog.* (Transl. M. K. Wilson.) London: Methuen. (First published 1954.)

Maccaby, M. (1976). *The Gamesman: The New Corporate Leader.* New York: Simon & Schuster.

Manchester, W. (1983*). The Last Lion: Winston Spencer Churchill, Visions of Glory.* Little Brown & Co.

Matusak, L. R. (1997). *Finding Your Voice: Learning to Lead.* San Francisco: Jossey-Bass.

McCullough, D. (1992). *Truman.* New York: Simon & Schuster.

Mead, G. H. (1962). *Mind, Self, and Society: From the Standpoint of a Social Behaviorist.* Chicago: The University of Chicago Press. (First published 1934.)

Miller, M. (1974). *Plain Speaking: An Oral Biography of Harry S. Truman.* New York: Berkley Books.

Murray, G. (1981). Kaichi Tsuji — *Zen in the Kitchen*. PHP, Vol. II, No. 10, pp. 39–44.

Niebuhr, R. (2001). *Moral Man and Immoral Society: A Study in Ethics and Politics*. Louisville: Westminster John Knox Press.

Pearce, J. L. (1982). Leading and following volunteers: Implications for a changing society. *Journal of Applied Behavioral Science*, 18 (3), pp. 385–394.

Peterson, C., Maier, S. F. & Seligman, M. E. P. (1993). *Learned Helplessness: A Theory for the Age of Personal Control*. New York: Oxford University Press.

Phillips, D. T. (1992). *Lincoln on Leadership: Executive Strategies for Tough Time*. New York: Time Warner.

Popper, K. R. (1999). *The Poverty of Historicism*. London: Routledge. (First published 1957.)

Presthus, R. (1978). *The Organizational Society*. New York: St. Martin's Press (Revised Edition)

Rapoport, A. (1986). *General Systems Theory: Essential Concepts & Application*. Cambridge, Mass.: Abacus Press.

Rovere, R. H. (1959). *Senator Joe McCarthy*. New York: Harcourt, Brace & Co.

Rudolph, S. H. (1971). Gandhi's lieutenants: Varieties of followership. In P. F. Power (ed.) *Meanings of Gandhi*. Hawaii: The University Press of Hawaii.

Ruesch, J. (1958). The tangential response. In Hoch, P. H. & J. Zubin (eds.) *Psychopathology of Communication*. New York: Grune & Stratton, pp. 37–48.

Russell, B. (1995). *Power*. London: Routledge. (First published 1938.)

Said, E. (1983). Opponents, audiences, constituencies and community. In H. Foster (ed.) *The Anti-Aesthetic: Essays on Postmodern Culture*. New York: The New Press, pp. 135–159.

Scheler, M. (1950). *Nature et formes de la sympathie: Contribution à L'étude des lois de la vie émotionnelle.* (Transl. M. Le Febvere.) Paris: Payot.

Sheridan, G. (1997). *Tigers: Leaders of the New Asia-Pacific.* Sydney, Australia: Allen & Unwin.

Siegler, M. & Osmond, H. (1974). *Models of Madness, Models of Medicine.* New York: Macmillan.

Smelser, N. J. & Smelser, W. T. (1964) (eds.). *Personality and Social Systems.* New York: Wiley.

Speer, A. (1995). *Inside the Third Reich: Memoirs.* New York: Galahad Books.

Sternberg, R. J. & Wagner, R. K. (1986). *Practical Intelligence: Nature and Origins of Competence in the Everyday World.* Cambridge, Mass.: Cambridge University Press.

Sternberg, R. J. (2004, July–August). Culture and intelligence. *American Psychologist,* Vol. 99, No. 5, pp. 325–338.

Stone, N. (1992, March–April). Building corporate character. *Harvard Business Review,* p. 104.

Sun Tzu (1983). *The Art of War.* New York: Dell Publishing.

Tolstoy, L. (1977). *Master and Man and Other Stories.* London: Penguin Books. (Transl. P. Foote.) First Published 1890.

Toynbee, A. J. (1987). *A Study of History: Abridgement of Volumes I–VI.* New York: Oxford University Press.

Verba, S. (1961). *Small Groups and Political Behavior: A Study of Leadership.* Princeton, NJ: Princeton University Press.

Von Bertalanffy, L. (1968). *General Systems Theory: Foundations, Development Applications.* New York: George Braziller (Revised Edition.)

Walizer, M. H. & Wiener, P. L. (eds.) (1978). *Research Methods and Analysis: Searching for Relationships.* New York: Harper & Row.

Weber, M. (1968). *On Charisma and Institution Building: Selected Papers.* Chicago: University of Chicago Press.

Weichert, F. R. & McFarland, D. E. (eds.) (1967). New York: Appleton-Century-Crofts.

Wrong, D. H. (1980). *Power: Its Forms, Bases and Uses.* New York: Harper & Row.

Zullow, H. M., Oettiingen, G., Peterson, C. & Seligman, M. E. P. (1988). Pessimistic explanatory style in the historical record: LBJ presidential candidates, and East versus West Berlin. *American Psychologist*, pp. 673–682.

Appendix I

Definitions of the terms "leader" versus "manager" obtained from four groups of managers from diverse professions.

GROUP A

Case No	LEADER	MANAGER
1	Always considers subordinates first. Dares to make decision in absence of fact.	Has a proper path to follow.
2	A leader is able to motivate, initiate something which others may follow. He may be a manager.	A manager has a leader's characteristics. It is important that a manager has a leader's character.
3	Provides strategic direction and guidance. Listens actively to staff grievances and pertinent issues and escalates reports to senior management to seek resolution.	Manages a team of staff.
4	Does the right things. Sets the vision and directions of the organization.	Does the thing right. Implements to achieve set objectives. The end justifies the means. Manages resources: time, manpower, materials, budget.

Case No	LEADER	MANAGER
5	A leader can be elected. A leader has followers to lead. A leader leads but not necessarily manages. A leader sounds lower-end.	A manager is appointed. A manager may have subordinates. There are sometimes managers without any subordinates. A manager manages. A manager sounds high-end.
6	A leader is not necessarily a good manager or one who can manage.	A manager can manage but may not have leadership qualities.
7	Visionary, authoritative, eminent, enthusiastic, veto power.	Planner, enterprising, obedient, cautious.
8	Manages the followers or supporters to do right things. Must possess good values in order to lead by example. Total commitment.	Encourages staff to do things right. Have good values but are assertive to carry out instructions. Committed during working hours.
9	A leader to me is always a manager in one form or another. Even in the most mundane activities, a leader will always have some form of managing to do.	A manager is not always a leader.
10	Provides the vision. Determines the where and the what. Needs to empower people. Sets direction. Takes risks. Takes uncharted waters. Develops and creates new ideas.	Plans and organizes the implementation of the vision. Determines the now and the when. Needs to motivate people. Implements direction. Manages risk. Sails on chartered waters. Produces ideas.
11	A good leader portrays a good manager but a good manager does not necessarily portray a good leader. He reflects credibility of the person but in a manager it reflects glamour.	A manager takes most responsibilities formally and requires training as a leader. Lack of leadership skills in the manager results in mismanagement and chaos.

Case No	LEADER	MANAGER
12	A leader is one who possess attitudes that others around him look to guidance, help and support.	A manager leads as well as : Plans: must have a vision beyond the immediate time frame; Executes: sets, tends towards getting things done and will not accept lack of action when it is needed; Controls: supervises, monitors and obtains feedback so that actions may be amended if necessary.
13	Not necessarily seen as a manager.	Manager must prefer development apart from the normal tasks.
14	Covers a broader perspective. Cares about the welfare of its (sic) employees. Concern about the long term objectives of the organization. Encourages a two-way communication betwoon all levels. Hold the good values of the organization.	Limited to specific assignments or tasks.
15	A leader is one who has the power to influence another person or group of persons in the way they exercise their choices. The power possessed by the leader is attained either by means of his social status, economy, political, religious, military or even charismatic charm. A leader is not necessarily a manager. A leader leads people; a single person without a follower cannot be a leader; whereas a single person could be assigned as a manager to perform specific function with allocated economic rewards.	A manager is one who is accountable and responsible for specific economic rewards (human, machines, tools, assets, etc.) For the purpose of specific objectives.

APPENDIX I
(Continued)

GROUP B

S/n	LEADER	MANAGER
1.	Direct or in control of.	In charge of / manages.
	Leads a group of people to work towards a set target.	Manage a group of people in achieving a set target.
2.	More aloof. Gives direction. Less personal. One who leads and commands. More in control of the situation.	Manages people. More people oriented. More group participation. Better ability to relate with people. In better position to listen to others and accept their views, spirit of team work.
3.	A person that commands respect through his charisma or exemplary performance. A person that others would like to emulate. Lead by example.	Command respect by virtue of position in the company May not be liked by all people concerned Strong ability in managing, coordinating and disseminating tasks
4.	More emphasis on <u>leading</u> a team or a group Still <u>manages</u> as a leader	More emphasis on <u>managing</u> and <u>organizing</u> Leadership is part of the role of a manager.
5.	Sets overall vision, directions & objectives Must be able to manage to achieve vision, to lead.	Follows overall vision given. May produce objectives etc. to achieve given vision. Not necessary to be a leader to be able to manage.
6.	<u>Active</u> Leads by taking initiative. Brings new ideas. Leads into uncharted territory. Inspires a team and gets results drawing out the best from followers. Strength of characters, man / woman of exceptional qualities who can rise above challenges.	<u>Passive</u> Reacts to situations. Applies tested solutions to problems. Works in a known environment. Just an overseer, not necessarily getting the most out of others. A man of routine who lives by rules and convention.

S/n	LEADER	MANAGER
7.	Extended boundaries.	Defined scope.
8.	Is concerned with "what to do", produce ideas, actively thinking of "what if". A leader need not be a manager.	Concerned with "how to do", thinks of ways to get work done, implementer of ideas produced by others. One can be a manager without being a leader.
9.	May or may not be associated with a business organization. Motivates people to achieve objectives. Usually concerned with long term goals.	Usually associated with a business organization Organizes and makes use of resources (include people) to achieve objectives. Concerned with both short-term and long-term goals.
10.	CEO, GM Focus on vision, planning – 5 yrs +. Appeal to the masses, company-wide.	Dept, divisional head. Focus on implementing objectives derived from mission – plan 1 yr +. Appeal to intra dept, divisions, at times even dept.

APPENDIX I
(Continued)

GROUP C

S/n	LEADER	MANAGER
1.	Inspiring. Innovative thinking. Communicator. Provide a balanced view to work and life.	Enabler. Coach. Ensure execution.
2.	A leader seeks the Vision / Mission & strategic direction of the organization. He is visionary. He thinks more long term. A leader also is required to manage but more on longer term requirements, strategic direction.	A manager devotes more time in running the area under his responsibility. Although some leadership is required, he tends to execute. Focus tends to be on short / medium term. Word used mainly in workplace.
3.	Forward thinking. Gives direction / structure / purpose to the team. Challenges the norm. Trains / grooms and builds bench strength in the organization. Fair and impartial.	Manages and guides a team.
4.	Set overall direction and vision. Lead by setting the tone for corporate values and culture.	Manages the resources available to achieve the direction and vision given. Motivate and drive the corporate culture.
5.	A leader is someone with a vision, intent to lead a group of people to achieve certain common goal and objective. A leader should have charisma and command respect of people and people are willing to follow his leadership. Able to motive people.	A manager is a task-oriented person who has certain goals or objectives and concentrate on getting subordinates to complete the tasks on a timely and efficient manner. He sets procedures and standard of work expected.
6.	Provides direction, goals & objectives. Visionary. Able to inspire and motivate.	Task-oriented. Plans, organize and coordinates. Executes objectives.
7.	A visionary with a mission to accomplish.	A person who fulfils and completes tasks assigned.

S/n	LEADER	MANAGER
8.	A leader must be able to set the vision and goals / objectives for the team. A leader however can be a manager as well. An illustration: For a team cutting a path through a jungle, the leader is someone who has the presence of mind to, once in a while, climbs up a tree to ensure that they are going in the right direction. The manager is one who instructs the team member "cut this tree, cut that tree".	A manager will, once the vision and goals are established, manage the deployment of resources towards achieving those.
9.	Visionary. Motivational. Inspires and drives change. Galvanizes teams.	Competent. Efficiency and productivity focus. Helps implement change.
10.	Has a clear vision to steer team to greater heights (moving target based on achievements and potential) Constantly maximizing resources to achieve greater benefits, even when targets have been achieved (constant revision of targets). Long term strategic views.	Maximizes best use of resources within constraints. May lack vision. May have short term, not long term outlook.
11.	Typically elected and recognized by the group as one. "Looked up" to by the followers / subordinates.	Can be in that position by appointment. May not necessarily "lead". May not be "looked up" to by the subordinates.
12.	Not everyone can be a leader. A leader must: a) have vision and clarity of focus, b) be able to convey / communicate vision / mission clearly, c) be able to lead without force or bullying.	All of us are managers. We manage: a) our own time, b) our financial resources, c) family; and d) even our superiors.

S/n	LEADER	MANAGER
13.	A leader is visionary and inspirational. His personal example is a key part of leadership. A leader has followers — the relationship is symbolic. A great leader is not necessarily a great manager.	A manager's role is organizational, not personal. He is the greasy mechanic who oils the wheels of business. Good management is more important to the business but good leadership is more exciting to see.
14.	Changes status quo.	Maintains status quo.
15	A leader sets direction and guides his staff. A leader usually does not tie the hands of his subordinates in following a fixed path of action to achieve the objectives set. He gives freedom to the staff as long as the objectives are met.	A manager ensures that the day-to-day-operations are met. Usually manages the resources to meet contingencies. Sets procedures and methodologies to carry out the day-to-day normal routines.
16	A leader is a manager and more. He knows the system and requirements. He is good coordinator. But more than that he has vision, is daring, and able to inspire people to work with him.	
17	Sets directions. Gives mandate to managers. Accountable for outcome of directions set.	Manager processes to achieve directions set. Exercises mandates given. Accountable for processes and variances of process outcomes from targets set by directions.
18	Leads by example. Inspires others by providing them with a vision and direction. Challenges the status quo. Could at the same time be manager.	Rules by the book. Assigns tasks to subordinates. Controls his people based on his position power. Follows rules and expects others to do so.
19	Has vision, boldness, pioneering spirit and leads his / her group through advising.	Good organizer. Skillful in holding his / her team together to work cohesively to deliver results and achieve goals.
20	Inspires vision and gives sense of mission, not just an administrator. Provides leadership.	Coordinator and administrator. Provides management and supervision. Manager / supervisor.

S/n	LEADER	MANAGER
21	A leader influences. A leader has followers. A leader has the responsibility of leading the team to a destination or towards achieving a vision.	A manager is more of an administrative job. A manager controls and organizes. A manager ensures the smooth running of the day-to-day operations of the organization.
22	Inspires. Concern with clarity of purpose. Wins respect.	Uses stick and carrot. Focus on getting the job done efficiently. Commands and controls.

Appendix II

This appendix contains a selection of verbatim responses. They are grouped in categories and subcategories according to the final classification system adopted by the author. The six broad categories are presented in alphabetical order. Responses within each broad category were further classified into narrower subcategories. Second order classification yielded 14 subcategories. These are presented in alphabetical order, each within its respective broader category.

CHARACTER QUALITIES

1. Achievement-oriented / Hardworking / Dedicated

Hardworking — diligent — dedicated — does not dump work on the staff — gets things done — works as hard as the staff — has serious view of work — has initiative — responsible in fulfilling his duties; a winner — successful — committed to the achievement of goals — efficient — disciplined — task-oriented — has initiative — does not have his head in the cloud — one who says 'let us do it' not 'you do it because it is your job' — go-getter — action-oriented — entrepreneurial — pragmatic — sets high standards — works harder and smarter than subordinates

2. Assertive / Strong

Assertive — firm — demanding when necessary — strong — strict — strong personality.

3. Courteous / Tactful / Considerate

Considerate — diplomatic — has pleasant disposition — has people relax and feel comfortable in his presence — not pushy — not overbearing — polite — respects subordinates — thoughtful — not bossy — respectful towards self and others — tactful — has an encouraging smile — has a kind word — does not order people around.

4. Energetic / Enthusiastic

Dynamic — enthusiastic — cheerful — exudes confidence — motivated — energetic — dynamic — acts with speed and energy — positive thinking — highly motivated — courageous — able to take calculated risk.

5. Mature / Stable

Confident — mature — avoids pointing fingers when things go wrong — clearheaded — cool — does not waver under pressure — flexible — manifests healthy attitudes — not temperamental (does not scold) — patient — possesses sound judgment — reasonable in expectations — self aware — has sense of humor — able to put his emotions under control — organized — reasonable — can deal with unusual situations — well disciplined punctual — all rounded personality — has common sense.

6. Religious / Spiritual

This is self-explanatory. It has not occurred at all in the list provided by Singaporean respondents and occurred rarely in the data provided by their Malaysian counterparts.

7. Sociable / Trusting

Cooperative — interacts well — able to mix with the staff — has good interpersonal skills — team player — trusting (of subordinates) — does not stay in the room looking old and tired and ready to die — finds time to mix with subordinates informally — good rapport with subordinates — cooperative — able to work with people.

COMMUNICATION QUALITIES

8. Clarity

Provides clear direction or guideline — sets clear and specific objectives — provides clearly defined roles and objectives — defines clearly the scope of different jobs — gives clear and concise instructions — communicates clearly and regularly — clear about his role as boss — sets clear priorities — seeks clarity — has clear vision — gives clear direction — gives clear instructions that can be easily understood — maintains vision and sharp focus — delegates duties with specific instructions.

9. Expressing / Transmitting

Open and straightforward — informs people about plans and change — shows future direction — responds to sound proposals — ready to give advice — good speaker — frank — communicates pertinent information — explains rationale — keeps staff informed — shares his vision and direction — shares company objectives — shares concerns with the staff — willing to impart knowledge and experience at all levels — able to display his emotions when the need arises — responsive — gives constructive feedback.

10. Receiving or Soliciting Information

Approachable — accessible — good listener — understanding — easy to communicate with — considers subordinates' opinions — has empathy — never says, 'I'm too busy I've got too much work' — willing to accept people's opinions — listens to arguments — receptive to proposals — welcomes and encourages new ideas — understanding — has empathy — available when you need him / her — able to listen objectively — lends me an ear — willing to listen to views of subordinates and to improve on them — accepts counter suggestions from subordinates — seeks views of subordinates — invites counter suggestions — solicits advice.

MORAL INTEGRITY

11. Accountable / Responsible

Has deep sense of responsibility — abiding by the rules and regulations — committed to organization goals — committed and able to see others' commitment to the organization — reliable — sees promotion as a reward not means to strengthen his circle — responsible — accountable for his actions — takes the blame for his decisions — bears the consequence of his decisions — defends the rights of staff — does not think only covering his / her back — does not shift blame — honors one's words — stands for his conviction — does not abuse his power.

12. Fair / Equitable

Fair — impartial — no favoritism — does not have preconceived ideas of any subordinate — does not discriminate — does not practice double standards — alert to status exploiters — impartial in appraisal of staff — fair in job distribution — does not exploit cooperative staff — treats staff equally.

13. Honest / Sincere

Honest — keeps promises — sincere — practices what he preaches — trustworthy — has sincere and unselfish interest in the organization — no back-biting — has integrity — admits mistakes — credible — has deep sense of honor — gives honest feedback — not self-serving — principled — righteous — selfless.

LEADERSHIP QUALITIES

14. Exercising authority
Readiness to take charge

Able to take tough action against 'black sheep' — able to exert control — bold in leading — able to lead — exudes great leadership — strong leadership — provides leadership — willing to lead — exercises his authority — possesses leadership qualities — firm in implementing discipline — provides guidance — assumes responsibility — has to be in control — leads by example — inspires authority — willing to guide employees — directive leadership — gives reasonable orders and directions — has leadership qualities — assumes responsibility — eager to provide guidance — effective leader — flexible but firm — manages and controls — provides leadership and direction — sense of ownership — strong leader — supervises and controls — takes charge.

Decisive

Ability to make the right decision — acts decisively once sufficient data is available — consistent; able to take a stand on issues; able to make unpopular decisions; executes decisions; thorough in decision making; firm in decision making; able to make sound decisions; quick in decision making; good problem solver and decision maker; able to make fast decisions; decisive; able to use judgment to solve problems; makes sound decisions; takes initiative; consistent in decision making; able to implement decisions.

Personal Influence / Role Model

Organization Ability or Managerial Proficiency

Able to advise on course of work — familiar with office procedures — familiar with guidelines, policies and procedures; coordinates — able to organize — able to distribute work properly and fairly; able to assign tasks to the right person — sets priorities; has good people management skill; reasonable assessment of the time required to complete a task — stabilizing — monitors well — creates a healthy work environment — able to promote a single culture in the department — able to unite the team — establishes good relationships among — junior officers — efficient coordinator — resolves conflict; has   managerial skills — provides motivational climate — able to maintain high morale — concerned with every matter.

15. Across-Boundary Management

Boundary spanning

Able to communicate to section heads — able to manage superiors — able to offer suggestions to top management — able to convince top management in making decisions on important issues; protects boundary — defends recommendations made when questioned by superiors — knows what is going on in the organization.

Boundary protection

Willing to back up his staff against outside parties when complaints are unfounded — willing to fight for and support subordinates — serves as an "umbrella" shielding one's mistakes from outside attacks and criticism — able to fight for and defend his unit — should not force subordinates to do jobs that should be done by other units — mediates.

Public Relations Involvement

Conveys messages to higher level officers — able to establish rapport between boss and subordinates; speaks up for subordinates — stands up for the views of subordinates — coordinates with other departments; good middleman between management and employees — mediates — respected by public — good public image— has good public relations — good PR — a team leader — develops team work.

16. Delegating / Sharing Power

Delegates authority and responsibility — allows subordinates to explore; does not interfere in any activities — sets objectives but allows latitude to accomplish them — lets subordinates take calculated risks; allows room for creativity; delegates the right job to the right person — incorporates subordinates' ideas — gets subordinates work with him rather than under him — facilitator not professor — trouble shooter — encourages the acceptance of responsibility — consultative — able to work in informal atmosphere.

17. Developer

Develops subordinates — mentor — willing to teach — provides development opportunities — facilitates — creativity — concern for career advancement of subordinates — provides development opportunities — allows freedom to grow and develop the organization — willing to share his expertise with subordinates — encourages career development — willing to teach — brings out the best in co-workers — shows what is wrong rather than who is wrong.

18. Recognition

Rewarding — recognizes good work — appreciates my contributions — gives praise for work well-done — gives due credit to deserving officers — recognizes potential recognizes staff's efforts — gives credit — differentiates well between performers and non-performers — rewarding — appreciative — makes you feel good about your abilities.

MENTAL EFFICACY

19. Expertise / Professional competence

Innovative; visionary; has foresight; [practices] contextual thinking.

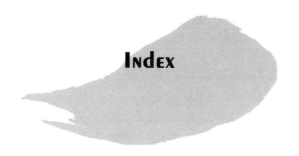

Index